"The human race
has one really effective weapon,
and that is laughter."

– Mark Twain

You Just Have To Laugh ... Again

How to Laugh When Life Isn't Funny

David Naster

Published by: You Just Have to Laugh Publishing
Lake Quivira, Kansas 66217 U.S.A.
WWW.NASTER.COM

All rights reserved. No part of this book may be reproduced or transmitted in any form or by any means, electronic or mechanical, including photocopying, recording or by any information storage and retrieval system without written permission from the author, except for the inclusion of brief quotations as a review.

Copyright © 2001
David Naster

First Printing: 2001 – March

Printed in the United States of America

Library of Congress Card Catalog Number: 20-011160

ISBN Number: 0966314522

Warning-Disclaimer

The purpose of this book is to educate and entertain. The author and You Just Have to Laugh Publishing shall have neither liability nor responsibility to any person or entity with respect to any loss or damage caused, or alleged to be caused, directly or indirectly by the information contained in this book.

You Just Have To Laugh ... Again

How to Laugh When Life Isn't Funny

David Naster

First Edition

You Just Have to Laugh Publishing
Lake Quivira, Kansas

Acknowledgments

I want to thank:

Hampton Stevens, my content editor and "Obe-Wan" of writing. His intelligence, insight and sense of humor made this project a joyous fellowship of laughter.

Diana Cooper, editor and typesetter. Her patience and care is worthy of sainthood.

John "Mort" Mortenson for his book design. Mort's remarkable mastery makes this book "look good."

Bob Gretz, the consigliere.

A personal thanks to my mom and dad for telling everybody they meet about my books.

> ***Thanks to all of you who constantly share with me your amazing ability to laugh in moments I would have never thought possible.***

Dedicated to my wife, Mary Ann

You make me be a better man.
(Jack Nicholson borrowed that from me.)

I love you with all of my heart and soul.
(Hallmark took that from me, too.)

Your never-ending support
made this project possible.
(Also ripped off by every Academy Award Winner.)

It was your eyes and laugh that clinched it for me.
(Okay, it was the house in Maui but you know how I feel.)

Thank you for giving me everything
I ever wanted in a relationship and especially
allowing me to completely be myself.
(Except for the flossing at the dinner table.)

English: You Just Have to Laugh

French: Vous juste devez rire!

German: Sie müssen nur lachen!

Italian: Dovete ridere appena!

Portuguese: Você apenas tem que rir!

Spanish: Usted apenas tiene que réir!

Table of Contents

Chapter One

Laughing When Life's Not Funny

"Life does not cease to be funny when something bad happens any more than it ceases to be serious when we are laughing."
— George Bernard Shaw

Since my youth, I have been drawn to the power of stories. My mother and father were always telling me and my siblings about our family's history or tales to teach us moral lessons. Sometimes they were funny, sometimes they touched our deepest emotions, but they were always meaningful.

I still love stories. As my parents knew, stories can teach lessons which offer a moral compass. Human beings are meaning seekers and stories can provide the insight we need to help understand ourselves and the world around us. Stories can also just be fun. While a good story may teach, a great story entertains while doing so.

I must admit, however, I tend to gravitate towards the entertainment aspects of a story — whether it has a lesson to teach or not. It is the presentation which excites me. I have always been fascinated by the bravado and charisma of a good storyteller. One of my favorite kind of storytellers was the old-time traveling salesman. Remember how he would roll into a drought-stricken village and try to sell the townspeople some magical device that would open up the clouds and bring rain. Even though his pitch was a bunch of bunk, it was fun to listen to.

The truth of the matter is folks, I am one of those old-time hucksters. The difference is, my stories are true and my magic device really works. Now, this device doesn't make rain, it protects you from it. I am referring to the shower of emotional troubles life can pour down on you. Unfortunately, nothing can stop those kind of downpours, but there is an umbrella which will offer some shelter during life's stormy times. That umbrella, that magical device, is laughter.

I take laughter seriously. I have to. I am a professional comedian, and making people laugh is how I have paid my bills for the last quarter century. I am also simply fascinated by what people find funny, and I often find it amazing that people have the ability to laugh at all — especially at their own lives.

Face it, there is nothing easy about being human. Just meeting our most basic emotional needs is no simple task. We all need to belong, to be accepted and loved. We all need a spiritual path that brings meaning and purpose to our lives. Trying to meet those needs, however, can make for an incredibly frustrating and complicated journey. Now add the burdens of plowing through an ordinary day: the frustrations of family life and relationships, the pressures of office politics, floods of e-mail, pestering, chirping cell phones, constantly rising medical costs — the list is endless. Heck, these days even a rush-hour traffic jam can create enough anxiety and anger to supply 10 years worth of guests for the Jerry Springer Show.

Unfortunately, the race of life is never over. There's always another hurdle to jump or deadline to chase. And to top it off, we can get hit anytime or anywhere with the three biggest obstacles of all — injury, illness and death. What could possibly be funny about any of those three? Plenty.

MEET TERRY GEDDES

"I was trucking down the highway in my old VW van when, from my rear-view mirror, I noticed fire coming out of the rear engine. I figured it was in the fuel line from the carburetor, but at that particular moment, I didn't much care where it was coming from. I just knew I had to put the fire out before I became a moving fireball. I figured, since I was at the top of the hill, I would have to get to the bottom if I didn't want to cause problems for other cars."

Terry never made it to the bottom of the hill. His car blew up and veered off the side of the road. That was in August of 1990. In October of the same year, Terry woke up from his three-month coma. As Terry lay in the hospital with third-degree burns over 60%

of his body and physically disfigured, he laughed.

"I never let up on the jokes," Terry says. "I told people I got drunk and fell asleep in a tanning booth or I was a tour guide at Chernobyl.

Later on, after the wreck, I was a roadie for the rock groups Steppenwolf and Commander Cody. While I was working with the bands, I had two favorite T-shirts which I wore all the time. One read, 'Patches' Crash and Burn Tour' (Patches has been my nick-name since grade school). The other read, 'I'm just a hunka-hunka burning love.' I have to deal with my life, so I just do it by laughing at it. It's really no big deal."

Terry is just one of the many people you are about to meet who prove that it is possible to laugh at in-jury. This next story proves you can laugh at illness.

MEET CURLY

After I gave a talk on the importance of humor, a bald gentleman in his fifties walked up to me. Smil-ing, he said, "David, I am a cancer patient. They call me Curly because I lost my hair to chemotherapy. Well, I wake up every morning and look at the paper to see if my name is in the obituaries. If it's not, I go on to work. I'll tell you this, you just got to keep on laughing."

It is even possible to laugh at death.

An elderly man had just died in his home. Family and friends formed a prayer circle around his bed holding hands. The minister began praying out loud for the dearly departed. Almost as soon as they began, the phone rang. The mourners ignored it and continued their prayers. Finally, the answering machine picked up the call. The pre-recorded greeting was, obviously, of the man who had just died. So, the minister's prayers were interrupted by the voice of the deceased saying, "I'm not here right now. I'm not sure when I'm going to be back. Leave a message and I'll get back to you as soon as I can." The prayer circle uncomfortably looked at each other then spontaneously broke out in laughter. That's when the healing began.

People give me stories like that all the time.

After the publication of my first book, "You Just Have To Laugh," I traveled throughout the United States and Canada on a series of speaking tours. Everywhere I went people came up and told me how they laughed to help get through troubling times. Hearing how people used humor during such serious moments inspired me to create another edition of "You Just Have To Laugh." The new edition, the one you are holding in your hands, is about how people laughed when their life didn't seem to be funny at all.

This second volume focuses exclusively on people

who found humor in the face of injury, illness and death. Don't let the subject matter fool you, these true stories are very funny. They also teach us a lesson: laughter not only provides immediate relief from emotional or physical pain, it also offers hope during what seems like a hopeless time.

It is my sincere wish that after reading this book, you, too, will be able to laugh at whatever trouble or trauma life pours down on you. I hope these stories of laughter will help break through any emotional clouds in your life and let the warm sunlight of brighter days come shining through.

As one of those old-time traveling salesmen might conclude;

"So gather 'round my friends! You are about to experience the enormous joy of a great story, the heavenly magic of the human spirit and the wondrous, redemptive power of laughter. Now, step right up and get some."

Chapter Two

You Just Have To Laugh ... Through Your Family Challenges

"A family that laughs together, grafts together."
— Naster Family Proverb

When families laugh together, they are creating an enormously powerful connection. Whether it is sharing joyful times during the holidays, telling funny stories around the dinner table, or simply watching a favorite TV show, laughing together creates a very special kind of bond. This bond can help a family endure the most serious of situations.

Be it the momentary crisis of a trip to the ER or the lifelong challenges of raising a child with Down's Syndrome, laughing together will make any family burden easier to bear.

TOTALLY BLAKE

Seventeen-year-old Blake Docking loves a spectacle. Be it a basketball game or Broadway musical, Blake loves the thrill of a big event, and his genuine excitement at these happenings always brings a gleam to his parents' eyes. In this way, the relationship between Blake and his parents is very much the same as any other parent-child connection. In other ways, however, the relationship is very different.

"When Blake was born," mom Susan begins, "the doctor told us he had Down's Syndrome. Unfortunately, that was not his only challenge."

Blake's dad, Gordon, continues. "He was a pretty sick little boy. He had some serious heart problems. At 20 months, he had open-heart surgery. That did the trick though, because ever since that operation he has been a very healthy kid. He is also a very happy and motivated young man."

Blake is the manager of his high school's varsity soccer team. The athletes and coaches love him and they respect the intensity and joy he brings to his job. So much so, they let him play in one of their games. For one of the home games, they insisted he run on the field with them as they made their grand entrance before the cheering crowd. Blake was so excited after this entrance that, as the team was silently facing the stands before the singing of the Star-Spangled Banner, he jumped out of line, turned to face the team and flexed his upper-body in an exaggerated "muscle-man" pose. The players were so tickled by his genuine enthusiasm they could barely contain themselves during the playing of the national anthem.

Susan talks more about her son. "Blake does not have very good language skills, but can still communicate very well. He kind of has a language all his own."

"It almost sounds like Cajun," Gordon interrupts with a smile. "But we understand him and so does his friend, Eric (a fellow teenager with Down's Syndrome)."

"When Eric and Blake talk to each other on the phone," Susan adds, "we can barely tell what they are saying — especially since we only hear one side of the conversation. Gordon and I will try to guess what they are talking about. It's fun for us."

"It's kind of like when Blake will be singing and dancing with his headphones on," she continues. "We won't know what he is listening to, so Gordon and I play 'Name That Tune.' We try to guess the song by what we hear him singing and see him acting out. Blake is such a ham! If he knows we are watching, he will really show off. It's a crack up! It's one of the many joys we get with Blake."

"Blake," says Gordon proudly, "is a really good golfer — and he really makes us laugh on the golf course, too. The first time we took him to a big, professional golf course he was absolutely thrilled. He got so excited, in fact, that after hitting the ball he just took off running after it — right down the middle of the fairway! Nobody ever explained to him that the etiquette of the game was to wait for the others to hit. It was funny, and it was just totally Blake."

"Another time, he was playing one of the best rounds of his life," the proud father goes on. "He was on the ninth green, and had a fifty-foot putt to beat his best score ever. Well, he stood over the putt and just smacked it way past the hole. Then he went over to his ball, addressed it, and again missed the putt by a mile. I couldn't believe it. I was thinking, 'What are you doing? You could have had your best game ever!'

But when Blake looked over at me with this great big smile, I figured it out. You see, Blake knew that when the ball landed in the cup on the ninth hole, it would be time to pack it up and go home. So he kept missing deliberately because he was having fun and didn't want to leave. He didn't care about getting the best score or winning. He just wanted to play the game."

The Dockings make a clear distinction between laughing at the infirmity and laughing at the things Blake does. They are not amused by Down's Syndrome. Down's Syndrome, after all, isn't funny. Blake, however, is.

"We have a child with Down's Syndrome," Gordon explains. We learned early on that Blake is Blake. He isn't 'normal,' 'ab-normal' or any other label. He's just Blake, and that's how we deal with him. We laugh about the things he and other kids with Down's Syndrome do because they are so honestly funny."

"It's the innocence that we find so charming," Susan says. "Once, at a Special Olympics tee ball game, a coach told a young girl to run down the first base line after hitting the ball. Well, she hit the ball off of the tee and ran down the first base line all right, past the base itself and all the way to the outfield fence. It was funny, cute and adorably honest."

Susan continues, "We know this kid with Down's Syndrome, we'll call 'Brian.' Well, when Brian was in middle-school, he not only attended classes, he also helped the custodians — and was good at it.

So, one day the school's electricity went out and no one could figure out the problem. Everyone had to be sent home until power could be restored. Later, they found the main power switch had been moved from the on/up position to the down/off. When asked about the switch, Brian said he had done it, explaining that he 'found the switch to the Bat Cave.' You see, the on/off switch looked just like the switch that opened the Bat Cave in the movies. Brian pulled the switch thinking he really was going to find Batman and the Batmobile. That's just funny."

Gordon continues, "Blake has made us aware of another world. We've met so many wonderful people that we would have never met if it wasn't for Blake. The bottom line is, he is a great person and we are very proud of him. We have learned much more from him than he has learned from us. He's the greatest teacher we've ever had or met."

Susan concludes, "We are a better family and better people because Blake is in our lives. Oh sure, it may get a bit hectic around here but we've learned to enjoy every moment and laugh. It's like that Jimmy Buffet lyric, 'If we weren't all crazy, we would go insane.'"

IF YOU KNEW KIKI LIKE I KNEW KIKI

Cathy Hamilton comes from a big family. She has 10 brothers and sisters. According to Cathy, all her siblings are very theatrical — mainly due to the influence of their Grandma Kiki. Kiki was a dramatic and flamboyant woman. She especially loved singing show tunes for her grandkids, and did so every chance she got.

"When Kiki was in her sixties she began experiencing the early stages of Alzheimer's," Cathy says. "She handled this frightening disease as she handled all of her problems — with her unique sense of humor.

If Grandma Kiki became lost in the middle of a sentence, she never panicked or got embarrassed. Instead, she would immediately start belting out one of her favorite show tunes. I still smile whenever I think of the time Grandma Kiki sang 'I'll Be Loving You Always.' It was definitely one of her most memorable performances — and certainly her loudest.

All of her grand, dramatic renditions of classic show tunes would have us in hysterics, and after every performance we would applaud and share a good laugh — including Grandma Kiki. The amazing thing was, even though Grandma Kiki sometimes lost her place in the middle of a sentence, she never forgot the lyrics to a single song!

Over the years, I have come to realize that Grandma Kiki wasn't only making herself feel better with her singing, she was helping the family as well. What was so amazing about this woman was that she knew what she was doing. Her performances defused the tension which surrounded her illness and that willingness to be silly and laugh at herself helped everyone get through a difficult time."

UNCLE LOUIE HAD A FARM, E-I-E-I-O

Jerry Bressel tells the following "tail:"

"My Uncle Lou has Alzheimer's. This past Father's Day, the family was talking and eating in the kitchen when one of the grandkids started singing 'Old MacDonald Had a Farm.' With every animal the kid sang out, Uncle Lou made the sound of that animal and repeated the name. When the kid sang, for example, 'On that farm he had some cows,' Uncle Lou would say, 'cows,' and then make a long, drawn-out mooing sound.

At first it seemed a bit annoying, even uncomfortable. Then we all realized that Uncle Lou was enjoying himself and not really doing any harm. We all kind of looked around at each other and smiled. Instead of being an awkward moment, it actually became kind of fun, even funny. I think that grandkid eventually sang the name of every animal on Noah's Ark — with Uncle Lou making the matching sound.

The song finally ended, the applause subsided and someone said to the kid who had been singing, 'Gosh, he sure did have a lot of animals on his farm.'

Then, completely out of the blue, Uncle Lou slapped the table, stood up and hollered, 'I don't give a damn how many animals Old MacDonald had! It's his damn farm and he can have as many animals as he damn well pleases!'

We all started laughing so hard, we practically had to pick ourselves off the floor."

GOD SEES EVERYTHING

Here's a story about laughter and faith from Rich Balot:

"I never got along very well with my older brother, Dave, but about two years ago we suddenly became the best of friends. Here's how it happened: Dave and I went together to a religious service for Yom Kippur. Yom Kippur is known as the Day of Atonement. It is the very special day when observant Jews reflect on the wrongs they have done in the past year and ask God to forgive their sins. It is an extremely serious, solemn service.

For some reason, Dave and I decided to sit in the front row that day; big mistake. Halfway through the service, Dave told me a joke. It wasn't an even particularly funny joke, but I started laughing anyway.

Now, laughing at a place of worship is a different kind of laughing. It is one of the those silent laughs where you don't make any noise, you just gasp for air — and that makes it even funnier.

Soon, I was laughing so hard it hurt. I couldn't believe it. There we were, in the front row of the synagogue on the holiest day of the year, laughing right in front of the rabbi. I was literally biting my finger to keep from laughing out loud and disturbing the entire congregation. My brother began laughing, too. We tried everything we could to stop, but the slightest sound or glance would make us break into silent hysterics every time. My best friend, Chad, even had to get up and walk to another seat because he started laughing as well.

At one point, a guest speaker began addressing the congregation, so the rabbi sat down for a few minutes — directly in front of me and Dave. The rabbi took one look at us laughing and then he started cracking up, too. For the rest of the service, the poor rabbi had to avert his eyes from us in order to keep himself from snickering.

After the service, several people came up and asked us what was so funny. We started apologizing, explaining that Dave had told a dumb joke and we just couldn't stop laughing. It turns out we weren't the only ones. One man told us his whole row had started laughing because of us. Then a woman said the same thing. It turns out several rows of people were laughing all the way through the service. The funny thing was, all these people were laughing and not one of them had heard the dumb joke.

That was the most fun I ever had in temple. More importantly, it was a real turning point in the relationship between me and Dave. Laughing together that day broke down some walls and helped us start communicating again. Today we are the best of friends. Whenever we go to temple, however, they don't let us sit in the front row.

A CELEBRATION OF MAHONEYS

When John William "Bill" Mahoney found out he had cancer of the bone, liver, pancreas, arms, head, legs and back he declared, "I got cancer every place but my lungs. I'm sure glad I didn't quit smoking."

According to his wife, Alberta, "The last weeks of Bill's life were times of celebration and joy. All our kids — Annie, Colleen, Maureen, Molly and Bill Jr. — appreciated Bill's sense of humor and celebrated it right up to his passing."

"Bill was always joking, even before he got cancer," Alberta continued. "In 1982 he was diagnosed with Hemochromatosis, an iron overload in the system. He would laugh as he told people, 'I have so much iron in me I can tap dance without tap shoes.' He also contracted diabetes around that time, but he never complained about giving up his Irish Whiskey and chocolates. He simply said, 'Just fix me what I am supposed to eat and I'll eat it.'"

Daughter Maureen remembered her dad joking during his years as an attorney. "I once watched dad try a case where a guy was being sued for emotional damages and a boundary dispute. The man who dad was representing had yelled obsessively at his neighbors. The jury clearly did not like dad's loud-mouth client and dad knew it. He had to win the jury over.

My dad approached the jury box and said, 'The laws of the United States are based on Common Law from England. There are certain ideas that have been passed down for hundreds of years which are still true today. One of these basic tenets of law is as follows: 'Stick and stones may break my bones, but words will never hurt me.' The jury laughed and dad won the boundary suit.

Once, after dad had become a probate judge, I went over to have lunch with him. The trial was running long, so I sat in the courtroom and waited. Dad saw me sitting there and loudly announced in the middle of the trial, 'Let the record reflect that daughter number three is sitting in this courtroom waiting for me.'"

Another daughter, Colleen, said, "Even when dad got sick with cancer he continued to joke with us. We would never want to leave his room. It was too much fun. One time he was looking at a blank wall as if it were a television and telling everyone in the room in detail what he saw. It was hysterical. He gave a play by play of a University of Kansas basketball game that took place in the 1940s. He insisted that we all be quiet while he described for everyone exactly what was going on. No one knew whether he was hallucinating or just kidding around. Then dad asked us, 'You can't see it can you?' I spoke up and said 'No.' He then looked at the wall and said, 'That's okay, it's gone now.'

'Sorry you missed the end,' I said.

'It's okay,' Dad said. 'We lost anyway.'"

Colleen continued, "We had hospice at the house so dad could be in his own bed. The whole family took shifts sitting next to the bed in case he needed anything or something happened. During one of Annie's shifts, she dozed off in her chair. As she was sleeping, dad fell out of bed. The sound of him hitting the floor woke her up.

'Dad, are you okay?!' Annie cried out.

He looked at her with a grimace and said, 'There are two reasons this happened. One, the disease and two, the caregiver.' Then he looked at Annie and smiled."

Annie picked up the story, "Another time, I woke up at 5:00 a.m. to find his bed empty. He had to use the bathroom and didn't want to wake me up. I found him on all fours trying to crawl out of the bathroom. He was too weak to go any further.

I asked, 'Dad are you okay? Can I help?'

He didn't even look up. 'Castors,' he simply said. 'I need castors. If I had them, you could just roll me back to my bed.'"

Maureen told of another time of trouble with a trip to the toilet. "Dad called out for help. Dan (a son-in-law) immediately went to the door, thinking something terrible had happened and asking what he needed. Dad called, 'I need paper.'

'Toilet paper?' Dan asked.

'No,' dad said, 'I want the sports page.'"

Maureen continued, "We would make a 'train' to get dad from the bedroom to the bathroom, living room or kitchen. Two of us would stand in the back and two of us in front of him. As we moved from room to room, dad would sing 'Chattanooga Choo-Choo' doing his famous two-step — the same two-step he did down the aisle during Colleen's wedding."

Son Bill Jr. added, "Another time, dad insisted there was a meeting going on behind one of the walls in his room. Dad asked Dan to quiet the meeting down. There wasn't any meeting, of course, but we always tried to honor his requests. Dan went over to the wall next to the china cabinet and proceeded to tell the 'meeting people' to quiet down. Dad looked over and said, 'Dan what are you doing? That's just the wall there.'"

"You never knew if he was teasing or not," Annie said. "One time mom asked dad if he wanted a cigarette. He looked at her and said, 'No thanks. I have one.' Dad then started smoking an imaginary cigarette, smiling and pretending to blow smoke rings."

"The Monday before Bill passed away," wife Alberta recalled, "he sat straight up in bed and said, 'Let's go out to eat.' I asked him, 'In your underwear?'

He said, 'I gotta get dressed. How about those fancy, new pajamas?'

I had to explain that he was too weak to go out to eat. 'Then let's go mess up the kitchen,' he said. After we put him in his good pajamas, we did just that.

Once we finished eating, Bill said, 'One is missing.' He was referring to Colleen, who had gone back to Dallas. We got her on the phone and Bill told Colleen, 'I'm going on a great expedition and I'm looking forward to it.' He then told Annie, 'I have a ticket. You can't go, because you don't have a ticket.'"

"Looking back," Annie said, "this was dad's way of telling us he was about to go. He had told me before about going on a great trip and that I couldn't go because I didn't have a ticket. He said, 'You had a ticket once, but you didn't use it.' He was referring to a time earlier in my life when I was very sick and we thought I might die."

Annie went on, "The next day he fell into a long, deep sleep. We continued to laugh, telling stories and singing at his bedside. Dad always loved to hear his daughters sing, so we would sing for him whenever we could."

The next day Bill Mahoney passed on.

"Even after he was pronounced dead," Annie said, "we weren't ready to let him go so we kept singing, laughing and telling stories. We grabbed a bottle of Irish Cream, passed it to each other and sang around his bed.

When the ambulance drivers came to take dad's body to the funeral home, we included them as well. One of the drivers called his wife to tell her he was going to be late. There was so much laughter in the background, his wife thought he was calling from a bar.

We continued celebrating dad's life all the way through the funeral. There was a big thunderstorm that day, so the service was held in a mausoleum at the cemetery. Once the service concluded, everybody rushed off to their cars. After almost everyone was gone, mom called us kids back to the gravesite to have us sing dad's favorite song, 'Hi-Lili-Hi-Lo.' I don't know how we got through it, but we sang at the top of our lungs."

Molly said, "The last three weeks of dad's life were a party — and he orchestrated the whole thing. He was a non-stop monologue of teasing and fun."

Wife Alberta softly concludes, "Bill did it all for us. He loved me and our children very much. He never said good-bye to any of us. He didn't have to. We all knew he loved us. That's why he kept us laughing."

IT'S O'DOUL'S TIME

Like Will Rogers, Bob Rowlands never met a man he didn't like. He would talk to anyone, anywhere — and make them laugh. Bob was a hit at every Rotary meeting where he spoke and could find the humor in anything. Even while dying of congestive heart failure, he literally laughed all the way to the end.

Johnny Rowlands, his son, flies a traffic helicopter for a network television station. Besides being an expert pilot, Johnny also understands that laughter is a gift. He inherited this perspective from his dad.

Johnny tells a story about visiting his father during the last couple weeks of his life. They were at his father's house, talking and laughing. Bob was bedridden and Johnny asked if there was anything he could do to help him feel better. Bob said he would love to take a nice, long, hot shower. Since he was so weak, though, he would need his son's help.

Johnny was going to have to get his dad undressed, wheel him to the other side of the house, help him into the bathroom and set him on a stool in the shower stall. But he was happy to do it. First he took off his father's clothes. Then, as he was unfolding the wheelchair, he heard a laugh. Johnny turned and saw his dad looking down at his own naked body and laughing.

"What's so funny?" Johnny asked.

Bob responded, "Who would have ever thought I would have ended up looking like this?" And laughed again.

While helping his dad into the wheelchair, Johnny realized that his father was so weak he would have to help him wash himself, too. That is, he was going to have to get into the shower stall with him. So, Johnny thought, it obviously made more sense for him to take off his clothes as well.

He helped his father into the wheelchair, took off his own clothes and started pushing his dad through the house, towards the shower. Then, spontaneously, they both started laughing. Here was this buck naked, 48-year-old man pushing a wheelchair with an equally naked 84-year-old man.

As the two of them made their way through the

living room, a cousin briefly knocked on the front door, then walked right into the house cheerfully calling out, "Anybody home?" Then, suddenly seeing the naked pair of men, the cousin froze into gaping silence.

Both parties simply stood for a moment, awkwardly staring at each other. The cousin was first to break the stillness, stammering out, "Th- th- this must be a bad time." Then quickly adding, "I'll come back later," while backing out and shutting the door.

There was another brief moment of stunned silence. Then Johnny and his dad erupted with laughter. "We laughed so hard," Johnny says, "it seemed like we would never stop."

Johnny continues with a story that took place two days before his father passed away.

"Because we knew the time was near, the family had all gathered around dad's bed," Johnny says. "Dad was very quiet, looking around the room at everybody. Then slowly a gentle, little smile crawled across his face. Soon he was fully beaming.

'Look at all of you,' he said softly. 'What a wonderful family ...'

Then he quickly became very serious. 'I'm ready to go,' he told us. 'But I don't know how to open the door.'

'Don't worry dad,' I told him. 'Go whenever you want. Selfishly, we want you to stay. But you should go whenever you think you are ready.'

Since I was standing at the end of the bed, I took his foot in my hand and started caressing it, asking,

'Is there anything I can get you? Is there anything you want?'

The whole family looked at dad, anticipating what his final request might be. We wondered what he would want — some sentimental object from his childhood, a memorable photograph, or possibly he might want to impart some final words of wisdom.

'O'Doul's ...,' he said softly. 'I would like an O'Doul's.'

We all started laughing. At perhaps the most intense and serious moment of his life, dad wanted a non-alcoholic beer. Of course, he would have rather had something with a little more kick, but he knew the doctors wouldn't let him have alcohol.

He was serious, too. He really wanted the beer. So, we got it for him. As he drank it through a straw, he started doing the same thing he always did — cracking jokes.

'Before you pull the sheet over me, make sure I'm dead,' he said. 'And when you cremate me, make sure I don't have a pulse before you stick me in there.'"

"That was dad," says Johnny. "He loved the attention and he loved making people laugh — all the way to the end.

I had a great relationship with my father. And as I look back on those final two weeks, and all the laughter we shared, I now think those were two of the best weeks of my life."

Chapter Three

You Just Have To Laugh ... at a Stressful Job

"A sense of humor can help you overlook the unattractive, tolerate the unpleasant, cope with the unexpected, and smile through the unbearable."
— Moshe Waldoks

Every job has stress and challenges. However, there are some occupations in which people must deal with illness and death on a daily basis. These extraordinary folks who choose to work in such difficult environments know laughter is truly the best medicine — both for those being cared for and for themselves.

I NEED A SNICKER

Mike Dittamore is a fire fighter and emergency room technician. Mike begins, "I joke around in the ER on a regular basis because I can do my job better with a light spirit.

There's this guy, I'll call him 'Tom' just to protect

my hide, who comes into the emergency room and lies about what is wrong with him. Tom is often abusive — verbally and sometimes physically. He usually comes in on his own, but this time he came in by ambulance. The paramedics told us, though, that Tom was waiting outside his house for the ambulance when it arrived. So, as usual, we had to wonder how sick he really was.

When he arrived, he was only wearing blue jeans. That's it: no shirt, no shoes — he still got service. Tom told us he had taken 10 baby aspirin, drank a half a bottle of liquid Tylenol and gulped two big swigs of antifreeze. We were mostly concerned about the antifreeze, because that will make you go blind and turn your liver into formaldehyde — you basically pickle yourself to death.

We could immediately tell by his symptoms the antifreeze comment wasn't true, but we were preparing him to check out the Tylenol and aspirin overdose. As he lay on the table, I asked him to put on the gown so we could begin some procedures. He refused and shouted he was cold and needed a blanket. I said we would get him a blanket, and again asked him to get in the gown. He refused — loudly. He insisted he wanted to be nude, then removed his blue jeans. I again asked Tom to put on a gown, but he wouldn't and, instead, began swearing profusely. He was screaming that he needed some food. He also insisted that he must have a blanket because he was freezing to death.

I looked him right in the eye and said, 'You know

pal, with all the antifreeze you drank, I figure you're good to about 20 below.' That made everybody in the ER laugh as they restrained and put the gown on him.

I was a little concerned about my comment because I heard some laughter coming from the other side of the curtain in the ER. I stuck my head in and there was a middle-aged couple waiting for treatment. I told them, 'I'm sorry if my antifreeze comment was a bit unprofessional.' Then I noticed that they both were still laughing.

The man spoke first and said, 'I would have laid the guy out and punched him, he was so rude.' The woman said that she laughed so hard she forgot about her stomach pains."

"Another time," Mike continues, "a woman came into the ER complaining of chest pains. The woman was very pregnant and reluctant to get into the hospital gown in the closed curtain area. She asked if there was a more private changing room. I said there was, but it was pretty far away and going down there, changing, then bringing her back would take too long. We needed, I told her, to get her into the gown and check her out immediately.

She again insisted she needed privacy because of her condition. I comforted her by telling her not to worry, that I see that kind of thing all the time. She asked if I worked with a lot of pregnant women. I said, 'No, my dad's got a belly bigger than yours.' The woman laughed, which eased her tension. Then she got in the hospital gown and we were able to help her."

"I am aware," Mike says, "that some find my comments disrespectful and unprofessional. I disagree. My comments are directed to the immediate situation and are always intended to reduce the tension. For example, I was once wheeling this elderly woman up to her room. She was fussy and kept complaining the entire way. Here's how the conversation went:

Woman: 'I'll probably have some stupid roommate.'

Me: 'I'll try to get you the bed next to the window.'

Woman: 'I'll probably be looking at a brick wall.'

Me: 'No, you'll have a very good view of the parking lot.'

Woman: 'What's so good about that?'

Me: 'Well, you can see all of the nice cars the doctors drive that their patients pay for.'

She laughed and quit whining.

Another time a patient in the ER asked if I was the doctor. I said, 'No, I work for a living.' The doctor, who happened to be walking in just as I made my wisecrack, immediately said to the patient, 'This is Mike. He *used* to be a technician at this hospital.' We all laughed and got down to business.

Once, I was drawing blood from a patient and noticed that she seemed very tense about it. I started violently shaking my hand and said with a smile, 'I'm kind of nervous. I've never done this before.' The patient was shocked at first, but her boyfriend got the joke and laughed. Luckily, she did, too.

Sometimes when I drop a patient off in their room, I'll say to their family, 'Your loved one is in good hands. Everything will be fine, but for goodness sake, if you want him to get out of this hospital faster, don't let him eat the meat loaf!' Okay, it's not my best line, but it always gets at least a smile.

You know, some people believe that if employees are laughing in a hospital, they are not taking their jobs seriously. Well, nothing could be further from the truth. I use humor and laughing to help make sure that I am in the best mental state possible for doing my job.

When I come to work in the ER, it's during a shift change and there is a lot of chaos. I will come in, turn up the radio, make a few jokes, hug a few people and then get down to business.

If I don't have this light spirit, working in the ER will pull me down quick. I can start my shift and immediately get demands for five EKGs, three patient transports, and any number of life-saving duties. If I am not careful, I can be in a bad mood in 20 minutes. Then I have a long 11 hours and 40 minutes to go.

For example, one time I walked onto a shift and a nurse said to me, 'We've been waiting three hours on this blood work. Nobody has drawn it. Go in that patient's room and draw it right now!'

Now I know she's mad and frustrated and she's just taking it out on me. So, instead of snapping back, I said, smiling, 'You know what I love about you? You're sassy!'

The comment stopped her dead in her tracks. She

looked at me, smiled and said warmly, 'Mike, you are such an idiot!'

Another time, I handed an X-ray to a doctor and asked, 'Is there anything else you need?' The doctor snapped back, 'What I *need* is for everyone to back off and let me do my job.'

Once again, I knew that though he was mad, he wasn't mad at me. So, I just took a breath and joked, 'You know Doc, I can take care of that. I am, after all, a technician at this hospital, so I have an awful lot of pull around here.' The absurdity of my comment made him laugh out loud.

I guess I am making the ER sound like it's all fun and games — far from it. One time, an ambulance called to tell us they were coming in with a two-month-old baby who was DOA (dead on arrival).

So, the poor little thing gets to the hospital and we ask how it happened. It turns out the father was lying on the couch, letting the baby sleep on his stomach. The dad fell asleep, too, and when he woke he found the child underneath him, suffocated to death.

It takes a lot to shut up a nurse or doctor, but after hearing what happened to that child, the ER became very quiet. The atmosphere in there was awful. I tried to think of something to say or do to ease the tension, but I finally decided there are some things you just shouldn't joke about — even though I knew a laugh would help.

It took almost two hours before anybody in the ER would even talk. Eventually, the staff started whispering things like, 'I just can't believe it,' and 'Can you imagine?' Finally, a few of us went to the break room to get some coffee. I still sensed we needed to laugh to ease the tension, and decided to trust my instincts as to when that time might be. After many gulps of coffee and a long stretch of silence, one guy finally spoke. He said, 'Can you imagine being that baby, and having your big ol' dad roll over and smother you?'

Here was my chance. I knew it was risky, but something inside me said this was the time. I said, 'I don't know about the dad rolling over on me, but did you get a look at that mom? She could smother me anytime.'

It worked. People snickered, and sometimes a snicker is as good as it gets.

You see, in an emergency room we see all the unimaginably gruesome and downright dreadful things that can happen to the human body. Sure it's a job, and we are trained to cope, but sometimes it gets completely overwhelming. A smile, snicker or laugh can be the only break we get during a grueling shift. So, I'll grab a laugh anyplace I can get one, because it helps me do my job better."

COMIC RELIEF

This poem is posted on the wall at Shawnee Mission Medical Center Emergency Room. Barbara Baldwin wrote it.

If you are waiting,
Possibly you may see us ... laughing;
Or even take notes of some jest,
But know that we are giving your loved one,
Our care at it's very best.
There are times when tension is highest;
There are times when our systems are stressed;
And we have discovered humor a factor,
In keeping our sanity blessed.
So if you are a patient in waiting,
Or relative of one seen,
Don't hold it against on our smiling,
It's a way to handle this team.

Sincerely,
The Team

DOWN LADDER! MAKE A HOLE!

Donna Reeves is a nurse. She was working in the critical care unit of a hospital which was undergoing a lengthy remodeling.

"First, let me tell you something important to the story," Donna says. "I love the movie 'Hunt for Red October.' I especially love it when the submarine captain yells, 'Down ladder! Make a hole!' and all the men flatten themselves against the wall. For some reason, that scene really tickles me. Ever since I saw the movie, I have always wanted to use that line. Well, guess what? I got my chance at the hospital.

There was a 'Code Blue' alarm in the emergency department. 'Code Blue' means there is a life-and-death situation and we must act immediately. I was closest to the stairs when the alarm went off, and so I started down as fast as I could. While racing down the stairs, I was bracing myself for a worst-case scenario. Suddenly, I saw a bunch of construction workers coming up the stairs. These guys were big and burly, and they were blocking my path.

'Down ladder! Make a hole!' I screamed.

The men jumped out of the way, flattened against the walls despite their tool belts, power tools and tool boxes. I guess they all had seen the movie.

I made it to the 'Code Blue' to assist in the emergency. It was a very difficult and draining resuscitation. After the situation was finally under control, I started trudging up the same stairwell back towards my nurses' station. As I walked up those stairs, I thought of how I finally got to use my favorite line from 'Red October' and smiled. Then I started thinking about the shocked expressions on those construction workers' faces, and how they flattened themselves against the walls. Soon I was chuckling, and the more stairs I climbed, the harder I laughed. By the time I got back to my station, I was in hysterics. The other nurses couldn't understand why I was laughing so hard after a 'Code Blue.' I told the story and then they started laughing as well.

I realized something that day: even when dealing with illness and death — no, *especially* when dealing with illness, injury and death on a daily basis — laughing really helps relieve the stress."

A LITTLE PAINT AND A LOT OF LAUGHS

When Bob Martin took over the Christ Villa Senior Retirement Home, employee morale was at an all-time low, patient depression was at an all-time high and there was only a 71% occupancy rate. By October the following year, occupancy had climbed to 97%. Here's how Bob did it:

"As soon as I got there," he says, "I told my staff, 'If you don't have a good time, I will fire you. It's just that simple.' I also made sure each paycheck had a personal message written on it — a funny thought, a word of encouragement or a compliment. I constantly told my staff to laugh and have a good time. If we laugh, I told them, so will our residents."

Bob continues, "The greatest problem faced by people running a retirement home is patient depression. Our patients are going from independent to dependent. That's a hard thing for anybody to deal with. They have to contend with the fact that their bodies don't work like they used to. What does still work, however, are their minds and their senses of humor. If they are laughing and mentally active, the depression stays low.

Laughter and humor are also crucial for keeping up employee morale. When we laugh, it brings us closer as a team. It lightens the load in a potentially depressing work environment. In our staff meetings, we share stories of the funny, real-life things that happen here.

For example, we had an 80-year-old woman who phoned the local postmaster, FBI, and police department because she insisted somebody was stealing her mail. When I went to talk to her, she told me she was hiding it, but people were still stealing it anyway. I asked her to show me her hiding place. She pointed to the trash can.

It was all I could do to not bust out laughing. I told her we would move her hiding place to a dresser drawer, convincing her that it would be safer. A couple of days later, she thanked me for the new hiding place, telling me it was working.

Another time, two residents were carrying on, shall we say, an 'intimate' relationship. The staff was concerned because the woman was beginning to suffer from the early stages of Alzheimer's. I approached the gentleman and asked him to put an end to the intimate aspect of their relationship. The gentleman insisted he was doing nothing against her will. I told him, 'Well, you have to understand she is getting Alzheimer's, and so she doesn't really know what she is doing.' To which the gentleman loudly replied, 'The hell she doesn't!' and gave me a big smile."

"Besides using more humor," Bob says, "I gave the whole place a face lift. In a storeroom, for example, I found all this paint which had never been used, so we gave the whole place a good going over. The colors were wonderful, and the new look made a major difference in the overall mood."

At the time of this writing, the Christ Villa Retirement Home is at 100% occupancy, and completely staffed without the use of a temp agency — virtually unheard of in the health care industry.

"I don't pay more," Bob said. "The secret is the laughing. Laughing is like the paint we used to fix-up the place — it's only good if you use it."

Recently, Christ Villa received the highest rating given out in over 10 years by the Kansas Department of Health.

A GOOD LAUGH WITH A GOOD HUG

Dr. Larry Lennon is a Clinical Psychologist in Carmel, Indiana. He also heads up the Family Bonding and Attachment Clinic, a facility dedicated to helping families bond — physically as well as emotionally and spiritually.

"It was in 1985 in Washington, D.C.," Dr. Lennon says, "when I saw how humor was used to coerce an inmate back into his cell. Threats of more punishment and physical force were not working. It was a social worker on the scene who solved the problem. She put a finger up her nose and pulled out a 'booger,' then started moving towards the inmate with the finger extended. The inmate was so repulsed that he backed right into his cell."

"We couldn't believe how well the booger trick worked!" exults Dr. Lennon. "It really shows how the use of outrageous humor can help deal with difficult patients — and I have never forgotten that. As long as you can say something with a little smile on your face and a twinkle in your eye, no one takes offense."

"One time," Dr. Lennon continued, "I was working with a very angry teenage girl. She kept throwing a book at my chest. Every time she threw it, I picked it up and calmly put it back on the table. Even though she threw it seven times, I refused to get mad. Finally, she got right in my face — an inch from my nose — and called me a 'm*th*r-f*ck*r.'

I still didn't get mad. I looked at her — still an inch from my face — smiled calmly and said, 'I know what you want. You want me to kiss you.'

She backed up instantly, saying I was a pervert and a psycho. The interesting thing was that while she was backing away, she also started laughing. My kissing comment threw her off — which is exactly what I intended to do. I had to break her rhythm of anger. Once that rhythm is broken, I can begin to help.

Another time, I was talking to a 17-year-old boy, but he wasn't answering. So I started loudly singing 'Kumbaya' — deliberately off-key. During my seventh time through, the kid screamed, 'Shut up! What's up with the singing?' then laughed.

I was treating a seven-year-old girl in a residential center for extreme violence. She tried to run away, both threatened and attempted suicide, attacked others and even smeared feces all over her room. I was holding her in a Trust and Bonding Therapy, but she shut down and refused to talk to me. I decided to go into my ventriloquist act. I would ask her questions and then answer for her. She eventually started laughing and talking."

"Let me tell you about another girl, Angelica," Dr. Lennon says. "She came to my clinic when she was 16 years old. A man had sexually abused her as a child. She was extremely angry, especially towards men. As a matter of fact, she hated men.

I wasn't getting through, so I decided to take a comic approach. Out of nowhere, I asked her, 'Why is a nose never longer than 11 inches?' Holding her angry glare, she shook her head to indicate that she didn't know.

I smiled and said, 'Because, if it was longer than 11 inches, it would be a foot!'

She didn't laugh at first. When she thought how corny the joke was, she smiled. I found the humorous approach worked very well with her. Eventually, we went on to do great things with her. Angelica is now a well-adjusted, happily functioning 22-year-old woman."

"With adults," the doctor says, "the humor is different. For example, I once asked a mother with four kids who the father was. She sheepishly looked down and said each child had a different father. All I said was, 'Wow, you have been busy!' She started to laugh.

I'll also use these techniques in my sessions with couples. Using humor and lighthearted teasing can help rebuild the bonds between troubled partners. I'll sometimes start sessions by asking couples if they ever read the book 'Men are From Mars ... (and they generally start nodding) ... and Women are From Hell.' They suddenly stop nodding and the men usually laugh. I, of course, act like I made a mistake. Then I will make a joke at the men's expense, just to even things out."

"Humor works," Dr. Lennon concludes. "It connects everyone immediately, making things flow more easily. Laughter is a lubricant of life."

PIG PROOF

When Pat Rodgers started working as a police officer in Florida, she wore a necklace with a pig-shaped charm attached. She found it humorous for a police officer to wear a symbol of what is considered a derogatory name for the police.

Wearing her piggy pendant came in handy when Pat was working for the University of South Florida Police Department. A fight had broken out in an urban community and quite a number of kids were involved in the brawl.

When Pat stepped in to break up the fighting, one of the kids saw the pig charm and started laughing. He yelled to the other kids, "Hey, the pig is wearing a pig!" A bunch of the kids heard, walked over to look at Officer Pat's pig charm and then started laughing. The fight broke up soon after.

"I was one of the few female cops on that force," Pat says, "so, I had to find ways to laugh. Humor would combat any negative or sexist comments the guys might throw at me. While we were out on calls, we were all business and nobody ever made those kind of remarks. During the slack times, though, I would get teased a lot. It didn't do me any good to get mad. If I laughed, the situation was immediately diffused."

At another point in her career, Pat was stationed in Gainseville, and assisted in the investigations of Gainseville co-ed murders.

"I had to encounter some pretty gruesome scenes," Pat says. "I got through them by laughing. What are you supposed to do when you walk into an apartment and there is a female head on the mantle, and a headless body is propped on the edge of a bed with it's arms and legs crossed like it was casually sitting there? We joked and laughed. My God! You had to, otherwise you would go nuts. People don't understand what cops deal with all the time. It's the joking around that helps us get through it."

Pat continues, "Sometimes we would be called to a lake where there was a 'floater.' When people have been dead in a body of water for a long time, the body absorbs a lot of water and becomes severely bloated. One of the officers on the call might say, 'Oh look, here comes the Michelin Man!' (referring to the cartoon character of the tire company). We would laugh. It would distract us from the horror of what we saw.

Once, I was at the interrogation of a burglary suspect. It was a perfect setting — a dirty, old room with a single light bulb and a thunderstorm raging outside. One of the interrogating officers was questioning the suspect pretty intensely.

After repeated questioning over a long period of time, the officer got right in the suspect's face and started screaming, 'The Lord wants you to confess!' No sooner had the word 'confess' gotten out of the officer's mouth when a tremendous bolt of lightning struck the building. It scared all us cops pretty good, but nothing like it did the suspect. He immediately confessed to everything — even some stuff we didn't know about! Every time we relive that moment, we laugh our heads off.

Humor is probably the best distraction from the trials and tribulations any police officer goes through," Pat concluded.

THE RULES OF MOURNING

"Somber faces are not allowed at our church. You will laugh when you come to St. James. I write over 75 sermons every year and each one has something funny in it."

These are the words of Reverend Emmanuel Cleaver. Reverend Cleaver is pastor of St. James Church in Kansas City, Missouri. He also served two consecutive terms as the Mayor of Kansas City, and is prominent on the national political scene.

"People have homes and jobs they don't like," the former Mayor says. "They have to cope with the world every day of the week — and all of the things they don't like about it. By Sunday, their spirits are stiff and almost inflexible. It is my job to pull out the joy that is buried deep within them. I make sure that we all laugh and celebrate joy."

Even at the solemn occasion of a wedding, Reverend Cleaver uses humor to help ease any tension the bride and groom may be feeling. "People who are married," he will remark, "live longer than people who are not. There are statistics proving that single people do not live as long as married people. Now, contrary to popular opinion, that does not mean that marriage is a slow death." The audience, the married ones especially, will always break out laughing.

"Even when you attend a funeral at St. James," Reverend Cleaver continues, "you will laugh. Laughter breaks the flow of pain. Recently, I told this story at a funeral: 'A man was walking through the African wilderness. Running at him was a lion, so he jumped for a nearby pit. Just after jumping, he noticed a python at the bottom of the pit, so he grabbed a vine. A rat was gnawing on the vine — which happened to be a grapevine. The man knew the lion was above him, the python below and the rat was eating away the vine. So what did he do? He plucked a few grapes off the vine and ate them! You see, we have to enjoy what gifts we have, even when surrounded by danger, disaster and death.'

When people laugh at a funeral, it shows them one thing: you can laugh again. I know this is true. My own mother died in 1986. I have never known that kind of depression. It was the deepest funk I had ever been in. Even as a minister, I kept asking God, 'Why?' Why did He take my mother? I almost left the church. I almost gave up the ministry.

Well, Howard Creccy, a pastor and friend of mine in Atlanta, heard my mother had passed away and phoned to offer condolences. He used, however, a most unique approach. He began bragging that his sermons were working better than ever, and he was very happy. Creccy is a single man, and he started telling me of all the attractive women who come up to him after a service, saying things like, 'You are so handsome — I mean, you gave such a great sermon.'

Creccy and I started laughing. I never would have believed I could have laughed again. After that, I made sure humor and laughing were part of every one of my sermons. I never had used humor much before. Now, I won't do a sermon without it, because I have personally experienced its magic. Proverbs states, 'A merry heart doeth good like medicine.' My goodness, is that true!"

Reverend Cleaver talks about sitting with Bill Cosby and Hillary Clinton soon after Ennis Cosby was killed. "Bill was making us laugh," Reverend Cleaver says. "He was imitating his minister and how he did the exact same sermon every Easter. It hadn't even been a month since he lost his son, and he was laughing — and making all of us laugh, too! At that moment, I realized even more that laughter is a gift — and that Bill Cosby is a gift to us all."

When asked how long he thinks people ought to grieve after the death of a loved one, Reverend Cleaver says, "One day." He quietly explains, "Night lasts so long. Like darkness, pain and misery must also end and give way to morning, light and joy." Reverend Cleaver then quoted Psalms 30:5: "Weeping may tarry the night, but joy comes with the morning."

"One can drown in sadness," he says. "Laughing is the lifesaver. Let me give you an example: I was in a hospital room where a woman's father had just died. The woman asked her husband for some money so she could get something to eat.

Sensing the sadness and tension in the room, I looked at the husband and said, 'When I married the two of you a couple years ago, I thought it would take at least five years before she took all of your money.' They both laughed. The woman's father had just died, but she still found humor in the world.

Some may say I am being irreverent, but I am willing to violate some of the 'rules' of mourning in order to bring laughter and joy into people's hearts."

SENATOR DOLE IS A FUNNY GUY

The political arena is about as cut-throat a profession as it gets. Your personal and professional life is subject to a magnifying glass of scrutiny every day. Senator Bob Dole comments on how he has survived his successes and defeats.

"I've tried to master the use of humor," Senator Dole begins. "It brings people together. I remember many times in my years in Congress when things were tense and a wisecrack loosened people up." He continues, "I found the perfect way to deal with hate mail. I returned it to the person who sent it and wrote, 'Some fool sent me this letter and signed your name.'"

Even Bob's wife, Elizabeth, uses humor in the public arena. During the 1996 campaign, Elizabeth Dole appeared on "The Tonight Show with Jay Leno." Jay asked Mrs. Dole if she objected to all the jokes he was telling about her husband. Elizabeth replied, "Not if you don't mind being audited by the IRS after Bob is elected."

Shortly after his 1996 presidential defeat, Senator Dole went on "Late Night with David Letterman." David asked him what he thought about President Clinton's weight — due to the President's love of fast food. Senator Dole replied, "I don't know. I never tried to lift him. I just tried to beat him."

Senator Dole even mocked his defeat in a Visa commercial. In the commercial, Senator Dole eats at a diner in his hometown of Russell, Kansas. He tries to pay for his lunch by writing a check and a waitress asks the famous senator and local hero for identification. Senator Dole then looks into the camera and laments, "I just can't win."

DEARLY BELOVED

Chuck Bridwell was the minister who officiated the following marriage. As God is his witness, here's what happened:

"A couple of weeks ago, I was performing a wedding in my church," said the minister. "During the ceremony, there was a distraction in the front aisle. A man collapsed to the floor and a couple of other men started pounding on his chest. I immediately stopped the ceremony and asked the congregation to please be seated and remain calm (yeah, right). As they pulled the ill man into the aisle, I realized he was the bride's father. Along with the bride and groom, I went over to him. He was being tended to by two physicians who happened to be wedding guests.

The doctors decided he had not had a heart attack as everyone feared. Instead, he passed out because his daughter's wedding was too emotional for him — plus he had not eaten all day. We announced to the guests that he was going to be all right. Then I conferred with the bride and groom. They agreed that they wanted to continue with the ceremony and went into a back room to wait. I announced to the congregation the wedding would resume as soon as possible.

I went and got the bridal party to come back to the altar. Everyone took their places, but it was obvious to me that the bride and groom, the wedding party and the congregation were still pretty shaken up. Even though we knew the bride's father was going to be okay, you could still feel the tension in the room. I sensed it was my job to put everyone at ease and get the ceremony back on track. I decided to try a little humor.

Opening my prayer book, I cleared my throat and,

acting as if nothing significant had happened, I casually said, 'Anyway, as I was saying ...' The bride, groom and everyone else broke out in laughter. Everyone relaxed and we had a great ceremony."

I ONLY LIKE THE ORANGE ONES

LeAnn Thieman and Carol Dey were officers in the Iowa chapter of an organization called Friends of Children of Vietnam. FCVN raises money and collects supplies to send to Vietnamese orphans and adoption agencies. Whenever FCVN had six or so babies ready for placement in the United States, they sent chapter representatives like Carol and LeAnn to escort them home.

This trip would have special meaning to LeAnn and her husband, Mark. They had completed the paperwork for an adoption. Even though LeAnn wasn't planning to bring her son home on this trip, she would still be bringing children home for other families. That in itself was justification for the trip.

Traveling to Vietnam brought it's own unique kinds of stresses: a war-torn country, language and culture differences, not to mention the dreadful humidity they would endure. There were many funny things that happened on this particular journey, and they always seemed to happen when LeAnn really needed them.

LeAnn begins, "Before leaving, I had received a large blue duffel bag full of dossiers to be taken to

Saigon. These forms from adoptive parents would be used to assign homes to the orphans in the months to come. Since our dossier was in the bag, I guarded it with my life. In addition, I was given money — $10,000 to be exact — which was to be used for food and medicine for the children. I had been warned about muggers, hijackers and robbers we might encounter along the way.

'Great,' I thought. 'Like the pressure of carrying the dossiers and going to an unstable country wasn't enough, now I had to be responsible for $10,000 and hide it from potential thieves.'

I then proceeded to slip into a bathroom stall at the airport and began stuffing the money in my bra. I wasn't sure if I could fit it all into a 32B. When I finished, I could have put Dolly Parton to shame.

As I walked out of the stall, Carol's eyes widened and she burst out laughing. We both howled until tears streamed down our faces. We were bent over double, holding our sides, unable to stop though our ribs were aching. When we finally caught our breath, any tension we had about our journey had dissipated. We had strengthened our friendship and were ready for whatever lay ahead."

As soon as Carol and LeAnn arrived in Saigon, they headed straight for the FCVN orphanage. They were met by Sister Therese. Once inside the office, LeAnn announced to the nun, "Look what I've got!" and reached into her bra and began pulling out cash. The nun's eyes widened as LeAnn said, "My mom always told me to pin some cash to my bra for emergencies when I travel." Laughter filled the room.

LeAnn and Carol spent the next few days unpacking boxes and getting prepared to airlift 200 babies to the United States. Since they didn't know when their return flight to the states was going to leave, they had to be prepared to leave at a moment's notice.

Some of their work was packing airlift supplies in a warehouse behind the adoption center. It was a two-story metal building with huge rows of boxes — five tons worth. The heavy cardboard boxes were all covered with dust and mouse droppings. After five hours of rigorous work, the air was filled with dirt and feces which had been brushed off from the boxes. As the sun beat down on the metal roof, it was extremely hot and the humidity was becoming unbearable.

As Carol lay against a box feeling faint, she insisted what they needed was a sugar boost. LeAnn remembered some jellybeans which she brought from home and ran off to get them. When she returned, Carol was sitting on the floor resting her head against a box, looking quite pale.

"These will help," LeAnn said, handing Carol a fistful of jellybeans.

Carol looked up and whined, "I only like orange ones."

LeAnn dropped to her knees laughing and said, "You're sitting in a war-torn country, in a filthy 105-degree room, about to faint from lack of nourishment, and you only want the orange ones!?!"

Carol began laughing so hard she couldn't answer.

She gasped for breath as she draped her body across the dirty boxes for support.

LeAnn says, "The anxiety, pressure, and fears we faced getting those 200 babies out of a ravaged Vietnam was nearly insurmountable. Every time we laughed, it released the tension and kept us going. I am glad we did. My adopted son ended up being in that airlift."

READER ADVISORY

The following story does contain some graphic content that may be upsetting to some. It does, however, offer more insight on how EMTs and paramedics deal with the horrific things they are called to, on any given call.

BLOWING IT OFF

Chris Maltese worked as an EMT in New York City. He and his partners were called to a remote, desolate part of Queens.

"It was in the projects," Chris recalls. "We arrived to find a guy shot in the back of the head. As a matter of fact, most of his head was gone.

It was such an unusual sight that we stood around for a few minutes gazing into this guy's head, trying to figure out what everything was.

One guy decided it looked like an open watermelon.

Another guy said, 'All we need now is to get some

vodka and watermelon balls and put them in there.' Everybody laughed. Then, before we got in the ambulance, we began cleaning the brain matter out of our boot cleats.

Somebody remarked, 'Hey, it really is gray.' We laughed again.

Another time, we were dispatched to a subway. A train had hit a homeless man and we were sent to retrieve the body. When the train hit the man, his head was launched forward and his body ended up at the back of the train.

Since this was my first decapitation, I was a little nervous. So, to ease some of my anxiety, I called up front to the guy who had found the head and asked if it was a 'P' or a 'Q.' (There are some times when people die, their tongue sticks out of the mouth. When it goes off to the side we call it a 'Q.' When it sticks straight down, it is a 'P.') Well, the EMT wouldn't answer my question. He told me to just come up and see for myself. My partner and I got there to find the EMT sitting next to the head singing, 'I ain't got nobody.' We all laughed pretty hard at that one.

When you see crack babies die and so many youths taken by death, it can get to you. I used to get so emotional after seeing horrible things, I would punch the back of the ambulance with my fist. Laughing helps me blow it off. It makes it easier to go home, hug my wife and kids, and just make it through another day.

One time we were called to where a man had slammed his car into a tree. As I crawled through the back of the car, I suddenly saw the driver and let out a scream. The driver's neck had been broken, so his body was still facing forward but his head was turned completely backwards. My partner asked me if I was all right and I said, 'This guy gives a whole new meaning to eyes in the back of your head.'

When you go to a scene like that, or the others I've described, you are likely to see some extremely grotesque and frightening things. If you don't make light of it, you'll end up in a padded room.

All of our calls are approached in a courteous, compassionate and professional manner towards the patient, but when you go to a rescue and find the shell of what once was a living soul, you have to find a way to deal with it. That is why our humor is in private and not in public. You get hardened with the stuff you see, and I have found there is no better way to deal with it than laughing."

GUESS WHO?

Mark Conley is an air traffic controller who loves his job — and he is great at it! He had better be. Air traffic controller is one of the few jobs where you have to be 100% right, 100% of the time.

Mark begins, "Because of the concentration and pressure that goes with being responsible for so many lives, we grab humor wherever we find it.

Most of the time, it's sarcasm. We can get pretty sarcastic during our radio communications, but the playful words we use do not indicate a lack of seriousness. The wisecracks are just how we reduce the stress of such an intense line of work."

Here are some of those exchanges.

Denver Ground: "United 123, the good news is you are clear to taxi to Runway 16."

United 123: "Uhh, thanks ... What's the bad news?"

Denver Ground: "I don't have any bad news right now, but the sooner you get going the less chance there will be of my finding any."

***

Center: "Delta 123, say your speed for in-trail spacing."

Delta 123: "Oh Center, we're really hauling ass."

Center: "I don't care what kind of cargo you're carrying, I just want to know how fast you're going."

***

It was a foggy, busy "rush-hour" morning at LaGuardia Airport in New York. A USAir flight was taxiing to the runway when it made a wrong turn and came nose-to-nose with a United Boeing 727.

The irate ground controller (a woman) lashed out at the USAir crew, screaming and shouting on the ground control frequency. She ended her tirade with, "You can expect progressive taxi instructions in about a half-hour, and I want you to go exactly where I tell you, when I tell you, and how I tell you. You got that, USAir?"

The humbled crew responded, "Yes Ma'am."

The frequency went terribly silent, and no one wanted to engage the irate ground controller in her current state. Finally, after what appeared to be an eternity, an unknown captain from another airline came up on the frequency.

"Wasn't I married to you, once?" he asked.

***

Some local flying club students were visiting the tower for the first time and being shown all the equipment, radar screens, radios, etc.

One of the students asked, "Have you ever had a real live emergency?"

The controllers thought for a minute and then one replied, "Well yeah, we did run out of coffee once ... "

***

Approach: "UPS 123, expedite descent through four thousand and slow to one-seventy knots."

UPS 123: "Can slow or descend, but not at the same time."

Approach: "Did you just make that up or did you win that in your last contract?"

UPS 123: "Roger! UPS 123 slowing and descending!"

***

Overheard at Midway airport in Chicago:

Vanguard 123: "Midway Ground, Vanguard 123 push from Gate 32 with ATIS Bravo?"

Ground: "Vanguard 123, push back approved. Point your nose toward the city."

Vanguard 123: "Wilco."

Then, a couple of minutes later:

Ground: "Vanguard 123, just which city did you think I was talking about?"

***

It was very foggy in Billings, Montana. The visibility was between 800 and 1,400 feet all morning. Delta, Northwest, and United flights were waiting for departure.

One captain asked if any dramatic improvement was expected. The controller responded, "I don't think the weather's going to change much, but I'm expecting a dramatic improvement in about an hour ... when my shift ends."

***

Cessna: "Van Nuys Ground, this is Cessna 2467 Sierra, how do you read?"

Ground: "On about a twelfth-grade level."

***

On a very quiet Sunday morning, a pilot was flying his Robinson R22 helicopter to a very small uncontrolled field in Middletown, New York for a gathering of helicopter pilots for competitions and hangar flying known as a "Helicopter Round-Up."

The pilot's route passed through the Windsor Locks, Connecticut airspace, so the pilot called up and gave his location, altitude, destination and type. The controller cleared the helicopter into the airspace adding, "I used to work that district. What in the world are you going there for?"

The pilot replied he was going to Middletown to participate in a helicopter round-up.

After a lengthy pause, the controller said, "It must be kinda hard to lasso those puppies."

***

A few years BR (before radar), an "extra section" flight reported in to Washington Approach Control with a flight number that didn't coincide with any known airplane type.

The controller acknowledged and added, "Say aircraft type."

The pilot responded, "Ahh, wait one second ..."

The controller replied acerbically, "Whatsa matter? You gotta get out and look at the hubcaps?"

***

Heard on the frequency at Nashville, Tennessee:

Aircraft: "Hey, that altimeter setting we got put us 15 feet underground!"

Tower: "Well, up-periscope and taxi to the ramp!"

***

Airliner: "Approach, what's this aircraft doing at my altitude?"

Approach: "What makes you think it's YOUR altitude, Captain?"

***

The pilot of a small freight/mail plane was getting a little complacent in his phraseology, probably because of the rather dull routine of his late-night run. Every weekday at 2:15 a.m. he would stop at a small airport and check in with: "Good morning, Jones Field, guess who?"

The lone controller may have been bored, too, but he insisted on proper terminology. Every morning, he would lecture the pilot on proper radio technique. The lessons fell on deaf ears, though, and the pilot continued his daily, "Guess who?"

That is, until the morning when the radio crackled: "Jones Field, guess who?"

The controller, well-prepared, turned off all the airport lights and responded, "Jones Field, guess WHERE!"

From then on, the pilot used proper flight terminology.

***

The following are one-liners said over the air:

"Delta 123: You're gonna have to turn on your microphone. I can't see you when you nod your head."

***

"Southwest 123: Climb like your life depends on it ... because it does."

***

"TWA 123: If you want more room, captain, push your seat back."

Chapter Four

You Just Have to Laugh ... at the Military

"A POW camp is a microcosm of the world. The people who keep a light spirit and humorous outlook will succeed. The ones who face each day with the negativity of doom and gloom are going to have a tough time getting through it."
— Captain J. Charles Plumb, USN

What would it be like going to work every day knowing you could be killed at any time? The fine people who served their country in Vietnam understood that feeling. They used laughter as a shield against the emotional barrage of warfare.

A $25,000 COOLER

Hank Young is a world-class photographer. His work appears in major magazines all over the world. If you have ever picked up any of the better sports magazines, you have seen Hank's work. Hank was also a soldier in Vietnam.

"I studied fire direction control for artillery," says Hank. "My job was to figure wind, distance, and speed so that the artillery would be accurate. They first taught me with charts and pencils. Then they introduced the computer. We had one of the early lap tops. It appeared to be a fine piece of equipment, and was very expensive. All that was required for it to work properly was a 72-degree, humidity-free environment. Come on! There was no such thing as a 72-degree, humidity-free environment in Vietnam! So, the bottom line was, that computer simply wouldn't work.

What it did do, however, was provide us with a $25,000 cooler that could not be beat. You see, the computer sat useless in the corner, but the box it came in was front and center, keeping our beer, soda or water ice cold."

"I was in the 101st Airborne Division, Number 32, 1st Artillery," Hank goes on. "Our motto was: Fast, Accurate and Reliable. Little did I know, our speed, accuracy, and reliability would be used to make swimming holes.

If an infantry would be near a stream or river, they would always want a place to swim. We would shoot the first rounds over their heads, so they knew it was us. Then, they would have us fire 18 rounds of high explosive — at $87 a round — to blast out a nice, secure swimming hole; $1,566 for a swimming pool. There's a fine use of the taxpayer money.

Now, the M-16 rifle was my friend. It went everywhere I went in Vietnam, and it was one of the first things issued to me. After I served my hitch and it was time to go home, I was turning in all of my gear, but they wouldn't let me return my M-16 because it wasn't issued from the place where I was trying to return it. Now, some guys took them home as souvenirs, but I wasn't interested in that. Be it an enemy weapon or a U.S. issued one, I didn't want any souvenirs.

Finally I asked an MP what to do. One of the guys told me, 'You get yourself a shovel and you bury it. If it comes up, we'll just say it was lost on post.'

I explained to him it was in perfect condition and well-oiled. He explained to me my choices one more time. He said, 'Bury it or return it up north where it was issued.'

'Up north' was two days away. So I buried it. Hell, people even saw me burying it. But it's okay according to the military, because a lost weapon is a perfectly fine entry in a property book.

The waste was amazing, but we all said, 'Ain't no big thing,' or 'F-ck it, don't mean nothing.' As a matter of fact, that was what you said just to make it through the day. Be it on the battlefield, the hard times, the gruesome times — at any and all times, we would say, 'Ain't no big thing,' or 'F-ck it, don't mean nothing.'"

With a very unique look in his eyes, Hank tells how he dealt with the job of collecting bodies after battle. "The memories don't keep me up in the middle of the night, but I did laugh just to get through it. For example, we had a serious rat problem over there.

I remember setting the traps, eating our Spam sandwiches, and watching for the rats' eyes in the middle of the night. When we heard the traps go off, we laughed. That was fun and funny. It was that kind of stuff that got us through Vietnam. As far as the use of humor, here is my mission statement:

'War is the greatest waste of man and material that civilization has ever served up. Much has been written about the loss of life in war. I would never want to make light of people dying. To deal with death, I have used humor to the point of sacrilege. It doesn't mean a lack of respect for those who fell, only that humor was my tool for dealing with waste. As sacred as the human loss may be in war, the material loss will always be a hoot. Million dollar bombs for thirty dollar targets, parkas for jungle warfare, ice cream for lunch on 110-degree sand dunes. There are a lot of laughs in that stuff of the military.'"

NO SHAVING AND NO TOOTH BRUSHING

Captain Patterson would wake up every morning and scream, "VIETNAM SUCKS!" as loud as he could. That is one way he got through the war. In 1967 and 1968, Chuck Patterson was in the 3rd Marine Division, stationed at the DMZ (Demilitarized Zone). It also went by the nickname, "The Rock Pile." Captain Patterson describes his experience this way:

"Oh there was plenty of funny stuff that went on, especially because of Lieutenant Jeffery Maurer. This guy had a gift of gab; others might call it 'BS.' Jeff had a wonderful inventive mind, but he was a bit crude. He could talk for hours about anything to do with the female anatomy. Guys would act like they were interviewing him and, no matter the question, Jeff always found a way to bring the female anatomy into his answer. Sometimes his answers would go on for 15 minutes at a time! This may not sound funny to anybody that wasn't there, but it made us laugh till we hurt.

We lived in bunker tents on a base outside of a place called Quay Tri. Understand, in the military, we were always issued stuff that we didn't need. Once we got two foldable kayaks. Another time we got 10 gross of tennis balls. We are in the middle of the jungle of Vietnam! What are we going to do with kayaks and tennis balls? So we always traded stuff with other units — stuff we wanted, stuff we needed. One time we managed to finagle a 50-gallon drum equipped with a showerhead. The shower was a real blessing and everybody helped fill it up with water. The problem was that our Lieutenant Colonel got mad, because everyone not only showered, but they also shaved and brushed their teeth while under the spray. The Lieutenant Colonel insisted it should be for showering only.

Heck, we didn't care. We were the ones filling it up, but the Lieutenant Colonel didn't see things our way. He decided to have signs made. The signs were to be done up in Marine Corps colors — red and gold — reading, 'No Shaving and No Tooth Brushing.' The

Lieutenant Colonel's specific instructions were that the signs were to be posted by the shower.

The guys decided to have some fun. They took the signs and put them in front of the 'piss tube.' When the Lieutenant Colonel walked by and saw what the guys had done, he exploded with anger. He was screaming and hollering, throwing a temper tantrum like a kid. Watching his tirade over such an insignificant little joke made us laugh even harder.

Talking to the Vietnamese was another thing that made us laugh. We constantly tried to explain to them that they shouldn't use the rice paddy as a toilet — they should bury their excrement instead. One of our guys would patiently explain this and also illustrate by pretending to pull down his pants and make digging motions. Since none of the locals spoke English, they didn't have a clue what he was saying, let alone what he was doing.

We would roar with laughter, watching him and seeing their faces.

Laughing was our release. Once in Da Nang, we took a tank from the mobile construction battalion of the Navy. Not only did we take it, we offered tank rides to the locals. We charged 10 bucks a ride and made some serious spending money. That was pretty funny. We laughed a lot because we fought a lot. After hours — sometimes days — of brutal combat, your nerves get so frazzled that your emotions shut down. You block out the horror with laughter. Everything after that 'shut down' is funny. For example, we would see a body with no head and make a joke about it.

You had to, or you would go crazy."

EXCERPTS FROM: "FAITH OF OUR FATHERS"
by Senator John McCain

"Keeping a sense of humor was indispensable to surviving a long imprisonment without losing our minds, and most of us looked to find some humor in our experience. Many greeted the most difficult moments with a dark gallows humor, and we were always grateful for occasions to laugh about the embarrassment and absurdities of daily prison life. When we are asked today about our years in prison, many of us are apt to include in our account, 'We had a lot of fun, too.'

... the prisoners whose company we valued the most were those who could make the rest of us laugh at our circumstances and ourselves."

— John McCain, Vietnam POW

POP'S DREAM

The following POW in Vietnam chose to remain anonymous.

"Humor was an important part of our lives and helped us keep our sanity. Most of the stuff we laughed at were things someonc outside a prison camp might find weird. For instance, suppose your roommate was kept in stocks for weeks at a time and his ankles were open with a stinking infection. You might tell him, 'I wish you would change your socks. They stink.'

Daily, we carefully passed the latest news through the secret camp communication system: notes, tap code through walls, voice, deaf mute code between distant cells, etc. These messages went from room-to-room and camp-to-camp until all had the latest news. To get caught would mean lots of torture for lots of men. It was dangerous, but communication was our life blood.

Most of us were Navy and Air Force pilots in our 20s and 30s, but Richard "Pop" Keirn was older, he was in his 50s. (He was also a POW during WWII.) Pop was being held in a camp called the Zoo Annex. When we received the following message in our camp, it made us laugh for weeks:

'The Zoo is celebrating today. Pop Keirn had his first wet dream in four years.'"

DAMNED IF I KNOW

Rear Admiral Robert H. Shumaker, USN was a Vietnamese prisoner of war from 1965 to 1973. He tells the following stories about his experiences — and those of his comrades in arms.

"In May of 1967, my good friend Marine Captain Orson Swindle, an F-8 pilot flying out of Da Nang, South Vietnam, had completed 205 combat missions, and his tour of duty was over. He was to depart Vietnam for the U.S. in five days when he received a call from Operations saying they were hurting for pilots and asking if he would take one more mission. Orson told them he would, if he could lead the mission. But when he arrived, he discovered he was flying wing with a Major from Group Headquarters. Rather than make an issue, he went along with the mission. Well, the flight lead had trouble finding the target, enemy gunners were alerted and Orson was shot down and captured.

Orson was interrogated and tortured for several weeks during the long march to Hanoi. After arriving, he was called in for his initial interrogation at the 'Hanoi Hilton' (an infamous POW camp). The interrogator, who was apparently less than experienced, began by asking, 'Are you Air Force?'

Orson answered, 'No.'

He then asked, 'Are you Navy?'

Orson again said, 'No.'

The interrogator, getting confused, blurted out, 'Are you Army!?'

'No.'

Totally frustrated now, the interrogator screamed, 'Well then, why are you here!?!'

Unable to resist the temptation, Orson replied, 'Dammed if I know, I've been trying to figure that out myself for the last four weeks!'

That was *not* what the interrogator wanted to hear.

When Orson tells the story, he laughs and says the look on the guy's face was worth his punishment."

Rear Admiral Shumaker continues with another story of life for a POW:

“After a year of imprisonment in Vietnam, I got a cell mate who had a good sense of humor. He used to spend hours kneeling by the wooden cell door, peeking out through a tiny worm hole to view the outside world. Once, he jumped back in apparent surprise to tell me that the Vietnamese had brought 10 ‘whores’ into the camp to tempt us. Immediately, I sprang to the peek hole only to discover a line of Vietnamese women in their black habits with conical hats ... and each one was carrying a ‘hoe.’ They were the ‘hoe’ers.’

The same cell mate wanted to learn to play the piano. I knew a little bit about music, so I drew a three-octave piano keyboard on toilet paper with self-made charcoal. I also wrote out some musical scores. He’d practice on this ‘piano’ for hours at a time while I watched the door to be sure no guard detected us. At night we would roll up the piano and hide it in the wall.

One day, the POW next door to us tapped through the wall that he was a bit ill.

‘Probably that time of the month,’ he tapped.

My friend tapped back, ‘I’ll play you some cheerful music on my paper piano.’

A few hours later my friend tapped to our neighbor, ‘How’d you like the music?’

Without missing a beat, the neighbor tapped back, ‘Pretty good for ragtime.’”

A STADIUM FULL OF JOKES

Major Wesley D. Schierman, USAF tells the following stories:

"On the sixth of June, 1966, 16 U.S. POWs were taken from a camp in North Vietnam, hand cuffed, blindfolded, placed in trucks and driven in broad daylight — which had never been done — some 40 miles to Hanoi. The North Vietnamese had been threatening to execute the POWs as War Criminals, so many of us felt this would be a one-way trip. Even so, we were thrilled to be near another American, as most of us had been living solo for up to one year.

When the trucks stopped and our blindfolds were removed, we found ourselves in Hanoi Stadium. Thousands of screaming Vietnamese had filled the stands.

The silence among us was finally broken when a young Navy Captain, Ed Davis was able to express quite well what we were feeling. He said, 'Well, the Christians are here. Where are the lions?' As serious as our situation seemed, that comment had all of us laughing hysterically. It so accurately expressed our perception of the situation.

Later that evening, we were joined by 38 other POWs from the Hanoi Hilton. Then we were paraded through the streets of Hanoi to allow the Vietnamese people to demonstrate their hatred for us. Thousands of Vietnamese did a good job of that. We were cursed, spit upon, beaten, cut by rocks, glass, bricks and bottles. After about an hour of this, we literally had to fight our way back into Hanoi Stadium. As we fell to the ground, exhausted and spent, Navy Lieutenant Cole Black, who had only been a POW for a week or so, turned to his partner, and asked, 'Say, do you guys do this very often?' It hurt to laugh at the time, but I still chuckle every time I think of his comment."

BEN DOVER

Lieutenant Colonel Robert G. Certain shares his take on how humor was used at his prison camp in Vietnam.

"During the first night of my capture, I was being interrogated about the features of my B-52. It was December 18th and quite cold. For hours, I had been standing on a bare concrete floor in nothing more than my skivvies and a blindfold, with my elbows tightly lashed together behind my back.

To every question, my usual response had been, 'I'm a celestial navigator. I navigate over water only. Everything else is handled by a specialist, and I know nothing about it.'

One question, however, drew a different exchange.

The interrogator asked, 'Did you have quail on your airplane?' ('Quail' referred to the AGM69 decoy missile, part of the B-52's bag of tricks.)

'No,' I responded. 'The gunner had fried chicken and the co-pilot had roast beef, but I don't think anyone had any quail.'

'No, no, no!' yelled the interrogator. 'In the bomb bay! In the bomb bay!'

'No ...,' I said, 'the bomb bay isn't heated or pressurized. They would never keep food in there.'

At that point, a guard standing behind me hit me as hard as he could with the stock of his rifle, knocking me against the wall and to the floor. They immediately raised me to my feet and resumed the interrogation.

'Not bird quail!' the interrogator demanded. 'Missile quail! Missile quail!'

'I'm a celestial navigator,' I repeated. 'I navigate over water only ...'

They might not have had a sense of humor, but I did.

It was Christmas Eve 1972. I was in Room Four of the 'Heartbreak Hotel' section of the Hanoi Hilton with my new roommate, Fernando Alexander. We had both been shot down on the night of December 18th and the camp medic was making his first rounds since our capture.

When the medic and the guards arrived at our cell door, I was sitting on my bunk facing the door. Alex was in the narrow aisle. The medic inquired about our needs. Neither of us were injured, but Alex had an ongoing medical condition that needed some attention.

He asked the Vietnamese medic, 'Do you have anything for piles?'

The medic shot back a quizzical look, so Alex elaborated, 'You know, hemorrhoids?' Then gestured broadly at his backside.

The medic still didn't understand, so the guard

ordered Alex to show the medic what was wrong.

Alex and I exchanged a smile and shrugged our shoulders. Then Alex got up, turned around, bent over and dropped his shorts. The medic, with his nose turned up, reached out, carefully spread Alex's cheeks with his index finger and took a look. The horrified expression on the medic's face was priceless.

That was the last we ever saw of him."

BELT BUCKLE BLUNDER

Captain James L. (Duffy) Hutton, USN tells the following POW story:

"In July of 1965, I was assigned to the USS VAH-1, which stopped at Subic Bay on its way to Vietnam. While there, I ordered a personalized belt buckle, which was to be engraved with my name, squadron and NFO wings. I was told the buckle would not be ready before my unit left for Vietnam, so I planned to pick it up on the way home. Unfortunately, I was shot down in October of 1965 and captured. So, consequently, I never picked up my belt buckle.

Some time later, Red McDaniel and his NFO passed through Subic on their way to Vietnam. The NFO, who knew me, saw my finished belt buckle on display in the same shop and told Red that I was a POW. About five years later, Red was also captured during combat and joined our group at the Hanoi Hilton. I received a tap message on my wall that Red McDaniel had a message for me.

I tapped back, 'I don't know Red, but send the message anyway.'

The message was, 'Duffy, your belt buckle is ready to be picked up at Subic.'

It was stuff like that which made me laugh and kept me going."

Chapter Five

You Just Have To Laugh ... at Cancer

"Someone asked, 'Did you have colon cancer?' and I said, 'Well, mine was a little bit different, I had cancer of the semi-colon.'"
— Steve Allen

Is it inappropriate or distasteful to mention cancer and laughter in the same sentence? Absolutely not. While, of course, nothing is funny about suffering from a deadly and painful disease, humor can be an incredibly valuable part of dealing with the suffering that cancer brings.

Whether you have the disease, or are involved with someone who does, there is always a choice. You can let the situation control you — living in depression and fear. Or you can take control of it, and approach the illness with a positive attitude and find some joy wherever and whenever you can. The following chapter illustrates that cancer is a subject which can and, in some senses, must be approached with humor.

THE ULTIMATE BALANCE

Scott Burton spent years as a comic and juggler performing at comedy clubs, colleges and corporate events throughout the United States.

Scott begins, "My job is to make people laugh, to take them away from their problems and make them feel okay. Since a comic lives from job to job, I learned to prepare for almost any situation, but getting cancer is something you can't prepare for. For a comic, cancer is the drunk heckler in the back of the room who won't listen to reason, who screws up your timing and won't sit down and shut up. Even so, being diagnosed with cancer didn't stop me from being funny.

Laughter cut through the tension of being in the hospital and facing cancer. I remember the first time I made somebody laugh during my one-year battle with the disease. My brother was visiting me in the hospital after one of my first operations. I was explaining that they had also given me a prostate exam, and my brother was smiling sympathetically.

'Wow! My first prostate!' I told him. 'I heard it was weird, but ... I mean ... that was a whole new experience. Are they supposed to use a puppet?' The laughter from my brother was so genuine and free, it changed the face of all our conversations throughout the rest of my operations and chemo. Right then, I saw that humor was the key to drawing others closer to me while keeping fear at bay.

Part of surviving cancer comes down to fear — and

learning how to handle it. Fear is a constant for every human. It is what sets us off in search of humor. I laughed and exercised my humor whenever possible during my recovery.

While in pre-op before one of my surgeries, I was propped up on my gurney. As I looked around the room, it occurred to me that everyone was tending only to me. I suddenly felt like a Roman nobleman at the forum. Embracing this brief moment of regal splendor, I turned to an attendant and said in my best kingly voice, 'Fetch me the oncologist ... he amuses me.'

Later, when the anesthesiologist came to my gurney to poke a few needles in my arm, I asked if he didn't have something like one of those nicotine patches instead. When I was being led to surgery, I called out like it was happy hour at a bar, 'Catheters for everybody! On me!'

Using humor in frightening situations shows us all that being sick doesn't mean we can't still be human. For instance, after a pin was removed from my knee (my fourth surgery), the anesthetic left me with no feeling in my right leg. The simplest twitch would send my foot kicking out of control. So, for fun I would gather nurses and friends around my bed and say 'Watch this!' then let my foot go crazy. I was like a kid with a new toy!

Another time, I tried to convince a friend there was such a thing as nasal therapy. I said, 'As you drink a glass of milk, the doctor makes you laugh and the tumor shoots out your nose. They're still testing to and 2% will work. The hardest part is ctor who can make people laugh.' I realized that creating laughter during my cancer treatment wasn't just for me, but also for all the people who don't know it's okay to laugh at life's hardships. Laughter puts people at ease.

For example, I was sitting around my parents' dinner table and held up one of the last hairs left on my arm (due to the chemotherapy). I said to my mom, 'You see that? Once that last hair is gone, I am no longer qualified as a mammal. I'm going to apply for an amphibian citizenship.' Even when I looked in the mirror, I laughed at being hairless. All I could see was ET's homely brother.

Cancer is a crash course in coming to grips with your own mortality. It may sound odd, but not all people are fortunate enough to have that. And what they don't know is that once you see the profound seriousness in life, you can truly recognize the beauty of humor."

BJ THE GODDESS

Barbara Johnson begins, "I was diagnosed with metastatic breast cancer and began chemotherapy that same month. The biggest issue is just trying not to worry. The greatest pleasure is finding a way to laugh.

Each week, I received chemo for two to three hours through an IV (intravenous) drip. Generally, there are a couple of people having chemo in the room with me. These patients will talk, read and work puzzles, etc., to fill the time during their treatment.

One week, I was reading a very funny book and found myself giggling, snorting and chuckling. I kept trying to stifle my laughter so the other patients wouldn't think I was totally insane. All at once, I looked up and realized they were all eyeing my IV. I could almost read their minds. They were sitting there thinking, 'I want what she is having.' I left chemo that day about as happy as I could hope to be.

Baldness is a very sensitive issue for women going through chemo. For some reason, it never bothered me. I bought half a dozen wigs and thought I looked like a goddess in each and every one of them. One male friend said I was his fantasy — I could be a blonde, brunette or redhead — whatever he wanted.

Once, I spent a few days in Atlanta with an old friend. I had known her for 20 years and we had been through everything together — every fashion craze, every personal agony — everything. Except cancer. I was dreading taking off my wig in front of her, because I was afraid of how she might react. You see, I had maybe a dozen hairs left — maybe six on top of my head and six in the back. I thought my friend might react with grief, fear, hysteria — something dramatic.

I was wrong. The first time I took my wig off, she pretended to be horrified and squealed, 'Oh my God, BJ! You are so gray!' We broke down laughing.

A few days later I was staying with another dear

friend. While getting ready to take a shower, she handed me a towel and told me there was soap in the shower. Then she paused and a smile started crawling across her face. I asked what was so funny. She started giggling, and explained, 'I was about to tell you where the shampoo is!' We both busted out laughing like crazy. Nothing like good friends to bring you back to earth."

"I found baldness," BJ continues, "can be a great advantage. My support group howled when I explained my technique for avoiding long boarding lines for airplanes. As soon as the first-class passengers are called, I walk up to the ticket agent, pull off my wig, say, 'Chemo. Bad day,' and strut right down the jet way. I've gotten a few funny looks, but nobody has stopped me yet!

My hair is growing back now. It is short, curly and trés chic. Given what all my treatments cost, I refer to it as my '$100,000 haircut.'"

GOOD-BYE CANCER, HELLO HAWAII

Gary Leezack gets turned on by the weather. That is why he became a meteorologist. Gary is one of the most loved and respected weathermen on the Fox Television Network.

At a time in his life when all was going perfect, he announced to his viewers he had Extroskelatal Osteo Sarcoma. It is a bone cancer that spreads outside of the bone. Not only is this type of cancer rare (six cases a year in America), it is also one of the most aggressive cancers there is.

Gary begins, "It was hard to believe I had it, but I decided I was going to make it fun and exciting. I thought, 'What an experience I am about to have!'"

Friend Andy says, "Because of that philosophy, Gary never got depressed. He made sure his life would continue to be filled with excitement — as it always had. Since Gary has a passion for the weather, we set it up so he received faxed weather data every day in the hospital."

"I couldn't wait till 5:00 a.m.," Gary says, "so I could get to work on the weather. I wasn't going to stop living just because I had a tumor removed. I knew I had to keep living and enjoying my life."

Because of the highly aggressive nature of the cancer, chemotherapy was next in Gary's extended forecast.

"I made sure I was always laughing. Jeff Penner is a very funny friend of mine," Gary says. "He would constantly do impressions of people we knew and keep me in stitches. I watched the Comedy Channel and Saturday Night Live broadcasts non-stop. Laughter kept the positive attitude flowing. So did planning exotic trips."

"That's how Gary kept himself from getting too down or too sick," Andy says. "He gave himself a lot to look forward to."

Gary agrees, "It's hard to get sick and die when you know you're going to Hawaii."

Andy says, "That attitude helped Gary breeze

through it. He is now back to full strength."

"It was hard," Gary concludes, "but it was exciting. I thank God for friends and family. The cancer could come back anytime, so I make sure I appreciate every single day."

I CAN'T BITCH

Dr. Jenny Ashby is a dermatologist from Great Britain. Before the year ran out, she decided to get her money's worth from her insurance plan and go to her OB/GYN. They detected a lump in her right breast, but when the tests came back, it turned out she had a tumor in her left one. So Jenny decided to have a Bilateral Mastectomy.

"If a tumor has been discovered in one breast, there is a high percentage of a tumor appearing in the other," she explains. "So, I decided to have both boobs taken off."

Jenny continues in her characteristically dry, British style. "It is funny," she says. "I always worried one of my children might get cancer. I imagined that if any of them ever got it, I would wish getting cancer on myself instead. Well, it did happen to me, so I guess I can't bitch! That strikes me as awfully funny."

Unfortunately, Jenny's double mastectomy was not enough. Her lymph node tests came back positive for cancer, so she had to begin chemotherapy. "My husband and I decided it was time for a vacation, so we took a trip to Costa Rica," Jenny says. "Just because

I was about to begin chemo, it didn't mean my life was going to stop. I was going to continue having fun.

Once, just after I started my treatments, a woman came up to me and said, 'I am sorry you have breast cancer. I had it and it was the worst five years of my life.' I walked away from her laughing, thinking, 'Why in the world would you tell somebody that!?'"

Jenny continued with how she laughed during chemo. She said, "People would say 'Nice hair,' referring to my wig. They obviously didn't know what I was going through and thought I actually had a new hair-do.

I would pull my fake hair off and say, 'No, it's a wig. My hair is gone!' and have a good laugh.

Other times I would pound my chest and head, saying, 'I have the 'no boob, no hair disease!' I usually did this to people who knew I had breast cancer, but I also did it to some who didn't. It always made me laugh. That's what's important when one goes through what I did."

I DON'T HAVE TIME TO BE SICK

Dick Schulte discovered a lump in his breast while taking a shower. The cyst that was removed proved to be malignant.

Dick says, "I had just gotten custody of my two kids. My wife of 14 years, who I thought I would live with forever, left me to 'find herself.' If that wasn't bad enough, I had recently bought out my business partner and taken out a major loan. I think the stress got to me.

The doctor wanted to do a mastectomy right away. Since I now owned a major nightclub and it was the busy season, I needed to make money. I told him I didn't have time to get a mastectomy and go through chemo. I asked if I could put off the surgery. He said yes, so I guess it wasn't that serious.

A month went by, and another month went by. I asked if we could hold the surgery out until January. The doctor said, 'Okay, but not a day later.' Since my divorce was finalized on January 3rd and the operation was on January 9th, I told people I lost three boobs in one week.

Nobody even knew I had the mastectomy except my family and the girl I was dating. I only lost three days of work. Then, every three weeks I would get a shot of chemo and lose another three days. That was it.

Since my wife had left me, I didn't have time to be sick. I was always in the club getting things done. True, I had a mastectomy. I was going through chemo, but I had two sons to raise and a business to run. I had motivation. I didn't have time to lay in bed. Otherwise, I would have withered away. If I would have had a nurse, I would have just lain there calling out for more morphine.

I lost all of my hair. Even though I knew it was going to happen, it was just short of devastating. One morning at the breakfast table, I asked my sons if they wanted to go get a hair cut. They said no. I insisted we all go, but they again protested. So I said, 'Okay, I'll just do it myself,' and started pulling out my shoulder length hair. Because of the chemo, my hair came out very easy. At first they thought it was gross, but we soon had a great chuckle over it.

My sons would later go and get 'butch' hair cuts in honor of me. It helped that short hair was in style but they still did it for me. I went to the cheap hair-cutting places since it was going to fall out anyway. I would usually start pulling it out myself just to have fun. You have to add the humor just to help you get through it.

I explained my bald head to the people at the club with either, 'I lost a bet,' or 'I thought it was the style.' People didn't need to know what I was going through so I'd wear a baseball cap or just make a joke about my hair loss.

I've always made people laugh at my club. In my line of work, you see a lot of misery and unhappy people, so I try to make them feel good. That's another reason I think I got this cancer — to help people. A lot of women who find out I had breast cancer want to talk to me about it.

One time, a girl came over to my house to use my hot tub. We no sooner got in the water when she took her top off and asked me to feel her breast. I thought, 'Wow, this divorce thing is pretty good!' Turns out, she was asking me to check her. She thought she had felt something and was scared. Well, she was right. There was a lump and she had it taken out immediately. Thank goodness it ended up only being a cyst.

Unfortunately, I have lived around cancer. I saw my mom die of it. She smoked three packs of cigarettes a day since she was 12. She bragged on it. She loved to smoke cigarettes and drink coffee with the girls. Well, they found a big tumor in her back and gave her six months to live. She had a great sense of humor about it.

The day she was diagnosed, she quit smoking. I said, 'Mom they just gave you six months to live! Just keep on smoking and enjoy yourself!' She told me, 'No, Dick. I always wanted to see if I could quit smoking.' She did it, too. She never lit up again. I guess I inherited mom's attitude. I always seem to laugh at the tough things in life just like she did."

"After beating cancer," Dick concludes, "I'm much more laid back. I don't let things build up anymore. I listen to people a lot more now, too. You know, most people just want someone they can talk to — and laugh with. That's really what it's all about."

EITHER YOU LAUGH OR YOU CRY

TV journalist, Linda Ellerbee, wrote about her experience with cancer in the January 1993 edition of McCall's:

"Looking for humor in things is a skill that has gotten me through even the worst of situations. In 1992, I discovered I had breast cancer and needed a double mastectomy. Cancer is serious, but there are funny things about it, too.

That summer I bought some breast prostheses to use while swimming. Instead of fastening them to my skin with Velcro as the directions instructed, I simply inserted the prostheses into my bathing suit. When I came out of the water, one had migrated around to my back. How can you not laugh at such a thing? Either you laugh or you cry your eyes out.

Sometimes you have to give others permission to laugh with, or even at, you. When a friend went with me to buy a wig to cover the hair loss from my chemotherapy, we giggled at some of the truly silly-looking wigs we saw. Upset, the saleswoman said to my friend, 'You shouldn't be laughing. Your friend has cancer. This is serious.' I said, 'No, you don't understand. A wig is not serious.' And she said smiling, 'You know, you are right.'

It is something I've tried to teach my kids as well. When my 23-year-old daughter saw me with my bald head and no breasts, she said, 'You look just like a Buddha — without the wisdom.' We both howled. I think we are never braver than when we stand tall, look into the sun and laugh. Laughter may be a form of courage."

Chapter Six

You Just Have To Laugh ... at Your Body

"Anyone who takes himself too seriously always runs the risk of looking ridiculous; anyone who can consistently laugh at himself does not."
— Václav Havel

It is one thing to laugh at yourself when you might be going bald. It is one thing to laugh when you put on a few pounds or say something stupid at a social gathering. It is something else entirely to find humor and laugh when you are disfigured in an accident, when your face scares children or when you weigh over 400 pounds. The following people find a way to laugh at their bodies even though their bodies are nothing to laugh at.

A WINDOW TO THE HEART

When most people see comic David Roche on stage, they probably don't notice his great smile, jovial eyes or curling gray hair. That's because David was born with a cluster of tumors, comprised of blood vessels, marring the left side of his face. The removal of them left him scarred. He also has radiation burns which have permanently purpled his left eye.

Add an asymmetrical jaw, swollen tongue, a lop-sided mouth robbed of its lower lip, and you now know the face David Roche shows the world. He will, though, let you inside his heart — and that is where his beauty is.

On stage, David explains that the tumors which were attached to his face were diagnosed as benign. It was the removal of them and the radiation treatments that followed which disfigured and scarred him.

He also tosses off one-liners about his appearance: "Hey, not only am I president of the Face Club for Men, I'm also a client," or "If someone doesn't understand me, I'll tell them to 'read my lip.'"

"Thanks to body piercing and tattooing," David jokes, "it won't be long before a face like mine is a fashion statement."

He is serious, however, when he says his face is a gift from God. But he also jokes when he says, "It's one of those gifts where you say, 'Aw, you shouldn't have.'"

David continues, "Walking outside every day with people looking at you like a monster, you lose your right to privacy. I believe my disfigurement has taught me a universal message — forgiveness and acceptance for myself and others. No matter what religion or culture a person belongs to, I symbolize people's deepest fears — that there is something wrong with them. It's part of being human.

One time, after a public speaking engagement, a woman came up to me and wanted to commiserate over the public agony we both had to endure. Her ailment was freckles. When she told me that, I wanted to slap those freckles right off her face. I do understand about feeling different, though, and even the smallest trait can disable people with fear.

I use humor to reach those fears. Hilarity instantly opens a window into an event which has been closed by pain. It changes it from something terrifying to something all right."

THERE'S NO PLACE LIKE HOME

Imagine suffering from Cerebral Palsy. Mindy Goldstein does. She also never grew any taller than a towering 4'8". Nevertheless, despite all of these obstacles, Mindy still manages to find the humor in her life — especially in the forgetfulness caused by her Attention Deficit Disorder.

Mindy explained that she must take the exact same route to and from school everyday. If she doesn't, she can get confused very easily and possibly lose her way. Once, she got lost on the way home from classes at her local community college. Here's how Mindy tells the tale:

"I must have taken a wrong turn and suddenly I didn't know which direction led to my house. I looked left, then right, but couldn't remember which way it was. I turned at a light that I thought looked familiar, but I was wrong. I stopped to ask a house painter, then a gardener. I even stopped at an office building where I called my mother from a pay phone, but I couldn't tell her where I was, so she couldn't help me. Then, a stranger in the parking lot tried to give me directions to my house. That didn't work either. I ended up on some dead-end, country road. Finally, after getting help from two construction workers, a policeman and a very patient older gentleman, I was able to get to a familiar site and phone my mother who came and got me.

For some reason, I never got frustrated or angry. Every time I got lost, I started laughing. It's not like my condition takes me by surprise. I'm used to getting lost, so I guess I've just learned to find it funny.

When my mom picked me up, she said, 'Do you know where you are now?' I laughed and said, 'Yes, I think I do because I'm not in an office building, at a construction site or on a dead-end, country road. I am here with you, and I want to go home.'

I felt like Dorothy in the Wizard of Oz. I just wanted to go home. I didn't need a heart, or courage or a brain. I just needed that Wizard for directions or possibly a ride home in his balloon. Next time I leave my house, I'm wearing ruby slippers."

I GOTTA GO

A woman in her 70s explains, "You have to laugh at the fact you're simply getting older. One day, I was driving in the countryside in northern New Jersey. A policeman pulled me over for speeding. I was speeding, but didn't want a ticket. Who would? As the officer approached my car, I started moving rapidly from side to side. The officer noticed my movement and asked if I was all right. I told him I had to use the toilet, and a woman my age can't hold it very easily."

She giggled as she continued, "I didn't have to use the toilet, but I needed an excuse to get out of that speeding ticket. As I drove off, I laughed at my prank. The more I thought about it, the harder I laughed. Soon, after miles of laughing, I really did have to use the toilet! That made me laugh even more. Then I was laughing so hard, I went right there in the car.

Believe it or not, that made me laugh even more. I couldn't stop. I even had to pull over because I was hysterical. As a matter of fact, I laughed so hard, my teeth fell out onto my lap. Tell me you don't have to laugh at yourself."

BIGGER THAN A BUMBLEBEE

Dale Wright is from Greenville, Indiana. His true gift is his ability to laugh at his size. "I am 6'3" and a 'slimmed-down' 430 pounds," Dale says. "When the following incidents occurred, I was still at my previous high of 475.

When you are as big as I am, a simple thing like using a public rest room can be a major ordeal. Whether getting stuck in the stall or literally breaking the commode off of the wall, I have always found a way to laugh at myself and my 'weighty' problems."

Dale is an avid motorcyclist and belongs to a riding club. One morning, four or five members of his club headed out for a day-long ride. Dale was taking in the sights at the back of the pack when something pelted him right between the eyes. Then he felt a tickling feeling on his chest, inside his T-shirt.

"I took my hand off the throttle," Dale says, "then stretched out the collar of my T-shirt and looked down. It turned out a bumblebee had hit me in the head and was now crawling around inside my clothes. Immediately, I pulled in the clutch, hit the brakes, put the kickstand down and jumped off my bike as fast as I could.

I started to tear off my T-shirt, but the overalls I was wearing got in the way. So, I unfastened the straps, let the overalls drop to the ground, then pulled off my T-shirt and started jumping around like a mad man, trying to get rid of the bee. I was so worried about being stung, I didn't even realize I had stopped smack dab in the middle of the road.

So there I was; a half-naked, 400-pound man, jumping around in the middle of the road with overalls around his ankles. Well, I finally got rid of the bee and I am standing next to my bike, totally exhausted, wondering how far I had fallen behind the rest of the club.

As I turned around to look for my T-shirt, I suddenly saw two little old ladies sitting in a late-model Ford, staring at me in total disbelief. My bike was blocking the road, so I guess they had been watching me the entire time. I stood there for a moment, completely embarrassed, then pulled up my overalls and moved my motorcycle out of the way. As the ladies drove off, I waved. They pretended not to see me. After making sure the bee was gone for good, I got dressed again.

Well, I was standing next to my bike, getting ready to go, when the guys in the club rode up. They had doubled back to see if I was having mechanical trouble. I told them my bee story. They were laughing all the way through. When I got to the part with the little old ladies, the guys bust out into complete hysterics, falling all over themselves.

I knew what happened to me was funny, but I didn't think it was *that* funny. When I asked why everyone was laughing so hard, they told me they had just passed two little old ladies who were driving right down the center of the road at about 20 miles an hour, shaking their heads!"

SIT-DOWN COMIC

Paul Shryack was born with Cerebral Palsy. He is a 33-year-old professional comedian who uses the hand life has dealt him as the basis of his humor.

According to Paul, he has always been positive. In high school, for example, people were uncomfortable around him, so he would try to put them at ease by using humor. Ladies and gentlemen, please give a big hand for Paul Shryack:

"First off, people don't think I'm intelligent. They see me in a wheelchair, hear how I have difficulty talking, and automatically think I'm stupid. So, I make a joke about that in my act. I say to the audience, 'People treat me like I just graduated from the fourth grade. That's not true — it was sixth grade. I graduated with Jethro Bodine.'"

"Performing comedy has taught me to laugh at myself — both on and off-stage," Paul continues. "For example, one day I could barely get out of my apartment because of snowy weather. I struggled, wheeling myself to the local coffee shop, but finally made it in the door. I was very wet and cold, and all the people in the cafe were staring at me. I smiled and said, 'I feel sorry for those gimps that can't make it out today.'

You just have to laugh at yourself. I mean, I am a stand-up comedian. A stand-up comedian is supposed to stand up in front of people and speak clearly — neither of which I can do. Now, that's funny.

I'm lucky. I'm one of the few disabled people I know who have a positive outlook — and that is due to my family. I'll never forget when I was 10 years old. I had a penny collection, but because of my CP, I couldn't get the coins in the slots. Mom refused to help me. She made me figure it out on my own. I give my parents a lot of credit for my outlook. I definitely appreciate their constant love and support, but I am most thankful that they made me do things for myself. Learning to be self-reliant has helped me fulfill my dream of becoming a stand-up comedian."

Paul's persistence has paid off. As he sits on stage in his wheelchair, he takes total command of the moment.

"I just broke up with my girlfriend," Paul jokes. "She pushed me too far." He then will ask an audience, "How many CP guys does it take to screw in a light bulb?" He waits for an answer. Nobody replies. He smiles and says, "One ... but it takes 100 bulbs."

Even Paul's promotional material uses humor. His business cards read: "If you can't understand me, drink more beer." His brochure reads: "If people want to have a good time, I certainly won't stand in their way!"

Paul Shryack's ability to write jokes is impressive. More amazing, though, is the gleam he gets in his eyes when he is on stage and making an audience laugh. Suddenly, no one is feeling sorry for Paul, no one is making fun of him. Everyone is just laughing with him as he jokes about the hand life has dealt him. In those moments, Paul has no disability. He is just like anyone else — except funnier — and his humanity comes shining through.

Chapter Seven

You Just Have to Laugh ... at the Hand Life Deals You

"Humor shows the mistakes and frailties of human life. Laughing at life's worst moments helps us stand it."
— Reverend Robert Lee Hill

It is an unfortunate fact of human existence that some people are simply dealt a bad hand by life. It doesn't seem fair when children are born with debilitating physical or mental conditions. It doesn't make sense when someone — even the kindest, gentlest soul on earth — is struck by a serious illness or injury.

We may search for reasons or explanations, but ultimately the question is not why these things happen, but how we cope with them when they do.

The people in this chapter discovered a way to deal with the hand life dealt them: they laughed.

2-4-6-8, WHO DO WE APPRECIATE?

Curt was a high school student in Mason, Michigan. He was also the coach for his school's Special Olympic athletes. Curt had gotten fed up with the way the "normal" high school football athletes treated his Special Olympic kids. The football jocks were constantly belittling Curt's athletes — calling them names, making jokes at their expense. Curt knew he had to do something about it and he decided to take the humorous approach.

One afternoon, the high school football team was leaving the locker room, heading for the busses that would take them to an away game. Coach Curt had all his Special Olympic students waiting outside, next to the busses. The football players saw Curt's kids and naturally assumed they were part of the crowd waiting to cheer them on to victory against their gridiron rivals.

How wrong they were.

As the football players walked by, the Special Olympic athletes started yelling out — in a whining, singsong, baby-talk voice, "Normy, normy, normy." (This was to make fun of the football players for being "normal.") Then they repeated it, "Normy, normy, normy."

After a moment of confusion, the jocks figured out they weren't being cheered for — they were being made fun of. Realizing that turnabout is fair play, the football players got the joke and started to laugh. Then, the Special Olympic athletes laughed, too.

From that point on, because of the outrageous-ness of the special athletes' display and the football players' willingness to laugh at themselves, the tension between the two groups was gone and the teasing stopped.

PIECE-O-CAKE

The first thing Jim O'Hara said when he was diagnosed with Multiple Sclerosis was, "It could have been worse, it could have been a brain tumor."

That was April 29, 1982. Jim says he has never been bitter or lost his faith in God. "On the contrary," he says, "my condition has made my faith even stronger. I am especially thankful and grateful that it happened to me and not my kids or wife."

It all started months earlier when Jim's legs started feeling numb. They just weren't doing what they were supposed to be doing. According to Jim, he simply felt "weird." He really knew something wasn't right when he couldn't finish 18 holes of golf.

Jim says, "I woke up one Saturday thinking I was having a heart attack. I wasn't. The pain went away, but after a few such episodes, I finally went to the doctor. He gave me a couple of tests, then insisted I immediately check into a hospital. I asked, 'How about in three days?'

The doctor said, 'No, today.' I asked about tomorrow. The doctor insisted it be right now. I said, 'Doc, I'm getting the feeling you want me to check in today, am I right?'

The test they performed felt like nails pounding into my muscles — and the guy doing it seemed to enjoy it! Four days later, a nurse comes in my room and wants to give me a shot. I said, 'I have been lying here for four days, nobody has told me anything. Now, out of nowhere, you want to give me a shot. What for? What's going on? You're not going to give me a shot until I know what it is for.' She wouldn't say anything, and left.

Then, my doctor immediately came in and asked, 'Didn't the neurologist talk to you?'

'No,' I said, 'nobody has talked to me.' That's when he told me I had a form of Multiple Sclerosis. I wasn't familiar with it, so I asked what it was.

He said, 'It shouldn't be too bad, a lot of people have it. It comes and it goes. I wouldn't be too concerned about it right now.'

Three weeks later, while I was leaving the hospital, I asked one of the doctors about the worst-case scenario for an MS patient. He told me they sometimes need to have a lobotomy. So, having MS was either nothing to worry about or I was going to get my brain removed. I thought that was hysterical, and I laughed my head off.

From that point on, it's been funny and it's been not funny. You just have to laugh at MS because it's such a stupid disease. I mean, I'm not sick. I don't hurt much, sometimes I hurt more than other times. Your body feels stupid. You wonder why you can't do what you want to do — and what you've done before.

It first starts off that you can't lift your foot. Then,

it moves to other parts of the body. Now, basic bathroom skills can't even be done. I know how to do all of these things, of course, but my body won't let me. When you can't do it, there is nothing to do but laugh about it.

One time, I was transferring myself from my chair to the toilet. Keep in mind, this chair I live in costs more that my daughter's car — and this baby doesn't have a radio, heater or defroster. Anyway, during the transfer, I missed my mark and ended up on the floor. Now, I can't get up, but I am lying there laughing. Why? Because it reminded me of that commercial, 'I've fallen and I can't get up.' I'm on the floor laughing, thinking I may be there all day. What a way for someone to find me — lying on the bathroom floor with my pants around my ankles — which is exactly the way my best friend, Howie, found me when he came over. It took a 911 call and the fire department to get me up and on my way.

My chair is the source of a lot of laughter. I had to call 911 another time — they know me on a first-name basis — because my chair got stuck in the way back position. When the police finally arrived, they took one look at me and started laughing. They actually said, 'What do you want us to do?' Laughing as well, I said, 'I'm not sure.'

We decided to move me into my manual wheelchair. During the transfer, my body began to spasm. So, the policemen are literally holding me down while I was shaking. I am laughing and the cops are laughing. That was a really funny moment.

It seems like a lot of funny things happen in the bathroom. I remember the time I taught Howie to use the crane which helps me get on and off the toilet. I taught him where to put the slings so he could lift me up. While swinging me through the air like a car engine, I saw the look on his face, and we both suddenly just burst out laughing. Howie said, 'Who else is going to do this, but your best friend?'

So I said, 'Okay, best friend, finish the job by wiping.' It was hilarious."

Jim gets quiet and begins speaking softly, "My faith plays a big part in the way I handle things. Far be it for me to understand God's plan or what God wants from me. I never blamed or got mad at God, either. I don't think God wanted to punish me.

When I pray, I ask God, 'If you are not busy, maybe you could take this away. I know you got a few more important things — like wars — to worry about, but maybe you could give me more strength so maybe I can handle this MS a little easier.'

We are all going to die from something. Sometimes I hear people say things like, 'He died before his time.' Well, I don't think so. Everyone dies when it's their time, not before or after.

I have never believed this is a punishment. I have never blamed anybody for me getting sick. It's just something that is. Like when the sky is blue — it's blue. And when it's cloudy and gray — it's cloudy and gray. There is no one or no thing to blame.

If I ever think, 'Why did this happen to me?' then I'm kind of implying it should have happened to somebody else. Why me? I don't have any idea. Maybe I got this disease to let other people know they can handle adversity. Heck, I don't know what the reason is. But I know I have a choice — I can be miserable about it or I can find a way to laugh. That's really the only choice I have.

My wife and I share a lot of humor. 'Piece-o-cake' has become our tag line. Anytime we accomplish a new task, we say, 'Piece-o-cake.' Most of the time it isn't, but once we finally figure it out, it becomes a 'Piece-o-cake.' Every time we say that, we laugh.

Laughing is what keeps me, my wife, and this family going — even though my humor gets kind of dark sometimes. Once, I suggested cutting off the body parts I can't use any more. I figured it would make me lighter to lift. Now that's funny."

KEEN INSIGHT

Cathy Hayes is a remarkable woman who has encountered great adversity and still keeps a fabulous sense of humor.

Cathy was 12 years old when she was diagnosed with juvenile onset diabetes. From then on, she had to watch her blood sugar carefully and inject herself with insulin. She developed complications from the diabetes and eventually lost an eye, but had it replaced it with a beautiful prosthetic one.

In 1990, Cathy had a brain tumor removed. The surgery affected nerves controlling the muscles in her face. With lots of physical therapy, she regained most of the use of her facial muscles, but the nerves controlling her functioning eye didn't regain their original capacity and it would not close completely on its own. Since there was a great risk of ulcers forming on the cornea, the eye had to be stitched part way closed.

None of these challenges has stopped Cathy. She can drive a car and is able to laugh about the challenges she faced in attaining her license. At the driver's license center, the examiner asked her why she wasn't reading the letters on the right side. Cathy explained that she was blind in that eye. The oblivious, bureaucratic examiner obviously wasn't paying attention. He said, "Well, why don't you just try it again."

Cathy laughed as she replied, "Okay, but I don't think anything's going to change." She passed the test.

Cathy went to school to become a medical technician in a doctor's office. As part of her training, an instructor asked the class to pair off and check each other's eyes to see that they dilated and contracted properly. Well, of course, the pupil of Cathy's prosthetic eye didn't dilate or contract at all. Deciding to have some fun with the teacher, Cathy and her partner told the teacher that something must be drastically wrong, explaining that her pupil wasn't responding properly. The teacher examined Cathy and was becoming quite alarmed before Cathy laughed and explained that the eye was prosthetic.

Another time, Cathy was visiting her good friend,

Jill. As they sat in the kitchen, Jill's husband noticed that the sun was shining in Cathy's face and offered to adjust the blinds. Jill realized that the sun was only shining on half her face — the half with the blind eye. Knowing Cathy as well as she did, Jill told her husband, "Aw, it doesn't matter. She can't see out of that eye anyway." Cathy laughed the hardest.

Jill says, "Cathy is amazing. Besides having the ability to laugh at her misfortunes, she is an avid quilter. Even with the loss of three quarters of her vision, she continues to create beautiful quilts. I am so fortunate to know someone with an unfailing sense of humor even in the face of tragedy."

STUMP THE BAND

Dick Solowitz is an actor with a flair for comedy. His comic timing is as good as it gets. His life, unfortunately, is not. Dick Solowitz is a double amputee. Because of diabetes, amputation was the only way to save his life. He now gets around by wheelchair and prostheses, and is fueled by sheer determination and a powerful sense of humor.

"People tell me to trust in God," Dick says. "I do, and that's great advice. But believe me, that's only part of the formula. I also want a damn good medical team!"

"Some call me a hero and talk about my courage," Dick continues. "It's neither. It's determination. I wake up every morning knowing that when I put my legs on, I am going to go through excruciating pain for the first few seconds. That's not a hero. I guess it requires some courage, but more than anything, going through what I go through on a daily basis requires determination — and the ability to find the humor in it all.

I didn't just suddenly get this sense of humor after I lost my legs. I grew up in a funny house. My family has always laughed — through the good times and the bad. Even at my dad's funeral, we laughed. A man with Parkinson's disease was delivering my father's eulogy. He read from the death notice out of the paper and his hands were shaking so bad he messed up the names and relations. This made Jim, my brother, and I laugh.

I whispered to my brother, 'I want this guy for my funeral.' Jim shot back, 'You'd better go before next Wednesday.'

That did it. We lost it. We laughed out loud at our own father's funeral. That's our family, though. We will always find humor at the most difficult times."

Proving the point, Dick spoke of his latest project. He is writing, and will star in a one-act play about his amputation. The play is to be entitled 'Stumped.'

"I have to do this," Dick says. "Look at what Christopher Reeve is doing. He played the Jimmy Stewart role in a remake of 'Rear Window.' He's even directing films. Everybody who is faced with a challenge has to find a way to keep working. That's why I am doing this project. It was either that or learn how to play seven instruments simultaneously and perform 'Stump the Band' on street corners."

Days before this book went to print, Dick passed away. The funeral was a jubilant celebration of his life. With Broadway music playing in the background and hundreds of helium balloons on the ceiling, friends and family told funny stories and gave touching testimonials to a man who brought the world great laughter and joy.

Some stories end more happily than others. Not everyone has to face what Dick Solowitz did, but all of us have to confront our own mortality, the fragility and unpredictability of our own lives. The question is how we choose to deal with those challenges. Dick Solowitz chose laughter. Because he made that choice, both his life, and the lives of all those around him, were far more joyful and fulfilling.

Chapter Eight

You Just Have To Laugh ... at a Crisis

"Here's another fine mess you've gotten me into."
— Oliver Hardy

Sometimes events seem to conspire against us. Sometimes life throws some pretty nasty curve balls our way, and we suddenly find ourselves wrestling with life-threatening situations. We never know how we will react to such moments until they actually occur. Some people might panic, some will get angry, some grow so depressed they simply become unable to take any action at all. The people in this chapter, however, took action. They reacted with humor — and humor helped them survive.

WRESTLING WITH AN AIRPLANE PROPELLER

Jack Newton was a professional golfer until he was hit by the whirling propeller of a Cessna 210. The 33-year-old Australian lost his right arm, right eye and half his stomach. He spent four months in the hospital — the first time. He's been through a dozen operations since.

"I was a mess," says Jack. "I'm lucky to be here."

"The pain was quite bad," he continues, "but I discovered the rehab patients that progressed the best were those who managed to maintain a sense of humor. That was a common thread. I figured I had two choices: sit in a corner the rest of my life and sulk, or get off my ass and give it a go.

My friends would come to see me, and they couldn't hack it. I could tell they didn't want to be there, so I'd make them laugh by cracking jokes. I would say, 'Wrestling with an airplane propeller is not something I'd recommend.'"

Today, at 50 years old, Newton tucks the empty right sleeve of his trademark blue blazer into the jacket's side pocket. With his bow tie completing the ensemble, he is a jovial TV golf commentator for Australian television. "I like wearing bow ties," Newton continues, "so I get the clip-on ones. And instead of traveling everywhere with this special device to cut my steaks, I just have the waiter cut my steak for me. I got tired of that bloody metal device setting off alarms in airports."

Not only is Jack Newton a respected TV commentator, he writes regularly for Australian Golf Digest. He jokes, "Writing is a tough, time-consuming craft, especially when you have a glass and cigarette in your only hand."

LAUGH — DON'T JUMP

Bill Veck was a legendary character in the world of baseball, famous for his wacky promotions and his farcical gift of gab.

One warm summer evening, while World War II was raging overseas, Bill Veck stood high up on the Wisconsin Hotel talking to Merv Connors. Connors, first baseman for Veck's hapless Chicago Cubs, was drunk, teetering on the ledge outside the hotel window and threatening to jump.

Very cautiously, Veck asked, "Merv, have I ever done anything unfair to you?"

"There's one thing I got to say for you, Bill," Connors said, staring down at the pavement far below. "You've treated me very well. Just beautifully."

"Then I'm entitled to ask you for one small favor, right?" Veck asked gently.

Merv glared distrustfully at Veck, certain he was going to try to talk him out of his scheduled flight.

Veck continued, anticipating Merv's suspicions, "No, I'd be the last guy in the world to stop you from doing whatever you want — our boys are in the far-flung battlefields of the world fighting for human dignity and the right of individual determination. But, don't you think you owe it to me to wait until I can call the photographers so they can get a picture of you hitting the sidewalk? You'd make every front page in the country, Merv, and the way things are going, we could sure use the publicity. Maybe you could change into your uniform while we're waiting?"

Connors emitted a short, appreciative chuckle — the only time Veck ever saw the man laugh. Then, without a word, Merv Connors climbed off the ledge and lay down on the bed fully clothed, dropping off to sleep.

MISS AMERICAN PIE

Schoolteacher and farmer, Rags Smith, tells the following story of a woman who found humor in one of nature's most frightening phenomenons:

"During the harvest season, out-of-town custom-cutters come to help bring in the wheat crop," Rags begins. "My friend, Jane, had one of these crews living in a camper-trailer behind her farmhouse.

Now, since it is Kansas, we are always on the look-out for tornadoes. Well, sure enough, one day Jane hears a tornado has been sighted, so she frantically gets her grandkids down in the basement. Then, she starts towards the camper-trailer because she knows the wife of the combine operator is out there. But, since the storm was coming so fast, Jane had to take cover herself. All she could do was pray that the woman in the trailer would make it to the basement.

The storm blew through, ripping up trees and damaging out buildings. Once it was finally all clear, Jane ran out to the trailer to see if the woman was okay. Well, it turns out she was just fine. The woman was sitting there in her trailer, eating apple pie right out of the pan.

Jane asked, 'My God, weren't you scared when you saw the tornado coming?' The lady said, 'Yes, I was. I realized I didn't have time to make it to the house, and I thought it might really be my time to go. So, I decided, I might as well eat pie.'

How's that for using humor to get you through a tough time?

Many times since then, that line, 'Might as well eat pie,' has run through my mind, and it never fails to bring a smile, no matter how bad the circumstances are. I use it on friends and family. No matter what the conflict or tension, I am famous for saying, 'Might as well eat pie.'

And you know what? It works every time."

YOU DON'T ASK A LADY HER WEIGHT AND AGE

Ginny Klempnauer was traveling south on Interstate-35 when her Honda CRX slammed into a truck. It wasn't just any truck, either. It was a double-semi carnival rig. The semi had shut off its running lights and was making an illegal U-turn because it was too long and weighed too much for the upcoming weigh station. Here is what Ginny says about the collision:

"I thought to myself, 'I'm going to die. This is it, I am going to need a body bag.' As the paramedics were hauling me to the ambulance, one of them asked my height, weight and age. I said, 'Somebody slap him. You don't ask a lady her weight and age.'

The paramedic said, 'Oh boy, we've got a live one

here.'

I said, 'Yes you do — and let's keep it that way!'"

Ginny was in intensive care for four days. She suffered multiple skull fractures and hearing loss.

"Oh, I'm not done," Ginny continues. "Two weeks after the accident, I had blood clots in my lungs and I found out both knees would have to be replaced. Did I forget to tell you my left tibia was broken, I had no depth perception, and my right ankle was crushed? What I am telling you is that I looked like The Hunchback of Notre Dame."

"I had constant headaches," she says. "I could predict the weather because my head would pick up any change of barometric pressure in the area. I also got a sixth nerve palsy which caused double vision, so I needed to wear an eye patch. The patch always seemed to scare kids — until I told them I was a real-life pirate. Kids would get a big kick out of that, and so did I.

I've always loved to laugh. I was determined not to let the accident turn me into a bitter, shriveled-up person who hates life. I held parties with the nurses in my hospital room, from 1:00 to 3:00 a.m. I made sure the Comedy Channel was on and we were laughing.

One day, I was talking with my daughter, when the physical therapist came in to start my treatment. Now, they had this triangle contraption rigged up so I could maneuver myself in and out of bed, but just before we began therapy, the therapist told me we weren't going to use the triangle apparatus. 'Today, he said, 'I want to concentrate on using some things you may have at your own home.'

Before he could say another word, I said, 'Oh, I have *much* better things than this in my bedroom alone!' The therapist started laughing. My daughter began blushing and got so embarrassed she had to leave the room. That made me laugh even harder.

There is one thought which has probably made me laugh the hardest throughout this whole ordeal. Every time I think about this, I still crack up. Not only was the driver of the truck stupid for attempting that U-turn, I later found out he didn't even have a valid driver's license. In fact, after the wreck, he had switched places with his buddy in the passenger seat to try and hide the fact that he was driving. I'm thinking, 'Sure, I may be partially disabled, but these guys will be stupid for the rest of their lives.'"

CAN'T NEVER DID NOTHING

Steve Palermo was an American League Umpire. On July 7, 1991 in Dallas, Texas that changed forever. Steve was finishing his dinner with friends at Campisi's Egyptian Restaurant when he heard that two waitresses were being mugged outside the restaurant.

Steve and his friends took off, checked that the girls were okay and started chasing the three robbers. They caught one guy and held him down, but the other two robbers ran to the getaway car, where a fourth robber was waiting for them. While the police were on their way, the three muggers doubled back in their car and fired five shots.

The first bullet hit Steve's friend, Terance Mann, in the chin and exited. The second bullet entered and exited his right bicep. The third hit Terance in the thigh and now rests in his abdomen. The fourth bullet ricocheted harmlessly off a wall, but the fifth bullet hit Steve Palermo at waist level. It tore a path through his body, bouncing off his kidney and smashing into his spine. Steve was instantly paralyzed.

"Stevie was immediately taken to Parkland Hospital in Dallas," wife Debbie says. "It is one of the best trauma hospitals in the country. Within hours of the shooting, I arrived at the hospital from our home in Kansas City and went directly to the recovery room. Stevie had just gotten out of exploratory surgery. When I saw him lying there, I grabbed his hand. He immediately opened his eyes, smiled at me and said, 'Hi Buckwheat,' (a term of endearment and nickname he has called me for years). At that moment, I knew we were going to be okay.

From the very beginning of Stevie's recovery, I made sure all of our family and friends did what they could to keep the atmosphere in the hospital room lighthearted. I remember there were some friends at the end of the bed watching the All-Star game on TV. Stevie was on an IV morphine pump. He could get a dose every 10 minutes if he needed it. Because of the pain and the morphine, Stevie was in and out of consciousness. He told me later that he woke up and saw his friends at the end of the bed, talking and laughing and exchanging money. These guys were betting on how many times he would use the morphine pump."

"That was just the beginning," Debbie continues. "Funny stuff went on constantly. Once, Stevie was being moved on a gurney. It stopped next to a nurses' station while the staff did some paperwork. There happened to be a big, bright picture of a clown hanging on the wall nearby. Even though Stevie was heavily sedated, he opened his eyes, saw the picture on the wall and said, 'Stop clowning around!' Then he immediately fell back to sleep. It was hysterical. I laughed so hard, I cried. As a matter of fact, for the next couple of hours, Stevie would wake up, make some funny, off-the-wall comment and nod off again. It kept us going for the rest of the day.

Corky Campisi, who owned the Egyptian restaurant, added more fun to Stevie's recovery. He would take orders and feed our family, friends and hospital staff. He would bring food and cases of soft drinks up to the hospital. The Campisi family wanted to make sure everybody was well-fed and happy. They knew surrounding Stevie with fun would help his recovery."

At this point in the interview, Steve looked at Debbie, smiled and said, "Is it all right if I talk now honey?" She laughed, and Steve started telling tales of his long and difficult rehabilitation.

"I remember one of the first visitors I had after I was shot was our dear friend, Robbie Lane. He brought me a box of sneakers, Air Jordan's to be exact. I told him, 'I can't wear those.' The next words Robbie spoke have never left me, and were an integral part of my recovery. Robbie said, 'Can't never did nothing.' That one really stuck with me.

There were these two kids, Cody, who was six years old and Mitchell, who was 10. Both had suffered severe head injuries. Cody fell off a horse and hit his head on a fence post. Mitchell got hit by a car.

We became good friends during our therapy. But believe or not, there was competition in those sessions. If I took 10 steps on a treadmill, Cody had to take 14. Then I would think, 'This kid can't do better than me,' and would take even more. Every time we walked places, he would race me. That competitive and playful attitude pushed us to recover quicker.

Both Cody and Mitchell visited my room often, always putting a smile on Debbie's and my face. They would come down to my room to watch baseball on TV. They would park their wheelchairs and get in my bed on either side of me. Debbie would go down and get treats from the nurses' station, and we would all watch the game — eating cookies and ice cream.

Cody and Mitchell would always make a huge mess and then leave. They thought that was hysterical. It made me laugh when I thought how these two kids, recovering from head injuries, were smart enough to leave the crumbs in my bed, while they returned to their nice clean beds.

We had so many people coming up to my hospital room that my brother, Jimmy, friend Raymond and

Debbie put a sign on my hospital room door that read, 'Doctors Only.'

Well, one time three men in suits came walking into my hospital room — two in front and one behind. Jimmy and Raymond jumped up to stop them and started to grab the two men in front. Thank goodness Debbie recognized the man in back before any grabbing went too far. It was George W. Bush and his two Secret Service agents. Since George W. was the owner of the Texas Rangers at the time and I had been shot in his jurisdiction, he was paying a friendly visit. Just thinking about Jimmy and Raymond jumping up to grab two Secret Service agents still cracks me up.

Even after I got out of the hospital, my friends never let up with the jokes. A buddy on the golf course said, 'Steve, I see you on 20/20. You're on all these TV and radio shows. I read about you in the paper. What's the big deal?' I told him, 'Hey pal, you get shot, you can get your name all over the place, too.' Joe Garagiola joked with me, 'Some of us Italians get shot and go to prison. You get shot and you get awards all over the country.'"

"You have to laugh to keep from crying," Debbie concludes. "I know laughter helped Stevie and I get through this very difficult time in our lives — and still helps us to this day."

READY ... AIM ... WAIT

Actor Norm Alden has been in movies such as "Back to the Future," "Ed Wood," and "I Never Promised You A Rose Garden." He is the national spokesman for AC Delco as "Lou the Mechanic" and has provided voices for numerous Disney animated films. Norm also knows that laughter can bring people together — even when tempers flare.

Early in Norm's career, he was a comedian and traveled all the time. During a long engagement in Oklahoma City — Louie's 29 Club to be exact — Norm made many friends and, after a late show, he offered to take a waitress friend home. She was too drunk to drive, and Norm wanted to make sure she got home safely. On the way, she told Norm that her husband was a light sleeper and the sound of Norm's car might wake him. So, she asked if he would drop her a block from where she lived. He agreed, not thinking anything of it.

The next day, Norm was lying out in the sun and fell asleep in his lawn chair. When he awoke, he was staring down the barrel of a shotgun. The man holding the gun started shouting, "I know you were with my wife last night! I saw you drop her off! I wondered why she had been coming home late every night! Now I know!"

Norm realized it was the husband of the waitress he had dropped off the night before. He cautiously asked the guy to relax and try to take it easy.

The angry husband continued, "I know you've been

sleeping with my wife! You didn't even have enough guts to drive her to the house! So, now I am going to kill everybody! I am going to start with you, then her, and then I am going to finish myself off last!"

Norm very quietly and calmly said, "Well ... that sounds like a plan ... but, why don't you start with yourself first?"

For a moment, the husband kept glaring like he hadn't heard a word. Then, he slowly realized what Norm had said, and started laughing. The man soon was laughing so hard he lowered the gun and ended up complimenting Norm on a funny line.

Norm concludes, "I have performed for a lot of people, but that's the best laugh I have ever gotten. Believe it or not, he and I actually ended up going out together for a beer."

BULLET HEAD

Traci Riehle worked for a company which provides long-term airport parking. One day Traci was shot by a disturbed co-worker — not once, but three times. When Traci realized she wasn't dead, she made her way to a shuttle bus. Not knowing if anybody else had been shot or killed, she drove to get help.

During Traci's months of recovery, her husband, Tom, helped her by keeping a sense of humor. When a television reporter asked for a picture of Traci, Tom gave her one of Traci in a tutu. When Tom visited Traci in the hospital and told her what he had done, all the alarms on her blood pressure and heart monitors went crazy. The nurses rushed in to find Traci and Tom laughing.

To this day, Tom calls his Traci "bullet head" and jokes that it would have been nice if they would have kept her jaw wired shut. She replies, "My voice is like a symphony to you and you know it!"

Tom says, "You've got cooler scars than me now."

Traci returns his smile and quips, "And I have a much better story than you'll ever have."

These days, Traci is preparing to go back to work. "The place I work at didn't shoot me," she says, "one man did. I realize I am not protected from anything. It's just called living life."

Traci continues to do just that.

FROM CHRIS TO SWISS

Chris Bailey was simply being a good Samaritan when he picked up three hitchhikers outside the "Wet & Wild" water park in Orlando, Florida.

"They were clean-cut kids in their late teens," Chris says. "We were laughing and having a good time, so I offered to take them all the way to Daytona. They kept asking if I was going out of my way. I said yes, but that I would still be happy to take them where they wanted to go.

The guy sitting up front with me asked if he could smoke. I said yes, so he lit a cigarette. Then a loud bang went off. (Later I realized that bang was a signal to the other two in the back seat.) Immediately, one of them wrapped something tightly around my neck, cutting off my air supply. My feet came off the pedals and the guy in the front seat started steering towards the side of the road.

We rolled to a stop on the shoulder. Then, one of the guys from the back seat got in the driver's side, pushing me to the center of the front seat. The other one slapped a pair of handcuffs on me and they drove about a quarter of a mile, back into a marshy wooded area.

As the car stopped, I suddenly remembered I had a knife under the seat. I was somehow able to grab it before they got me out of the car. One of them started pulling me into the woods and I stabbed his butt. I was so mad — with the adrenaline raging — I actually managed to break the handcuffs and pounce on him. Unfortunately, one of the other guys jumped on my back and it felt like I was being punched.

Actually, I was being stabbed — 16 times.

Overwhelmed and in pain, I could struggle no more. They covered me with swamp brush and tree branches, leaving me there to die. With the massive amounts of blood I was losing, I was barely conscious, but I could hear it when they started the car.

I distinctly remember lying there, thinking my life was at an end. Then I heard it — the car had gotten stuck in the mud. I began laughing. I thought of those three (jerks) panicking because they were stuck in a mud hole, and that made me laugh even harder.

After they finally got out of the muck and drove

away, I freed myself from the pile of brush and tree branches and started walking back towards the road. I constantly told myself, 'Keep moving,' because I knew if I rested for even a second, I wasn't going to make it.

Finally, I just collapsed. It was at that moment I suddenly saw the most unbelievable light. At first I thought it was a car, but I was still in the woods. The light seemed to fill my body, making me feel lighter, almost like I was floating. It was definitely a religious experience. The next thing I knew I was back on the road, in front of an oncoming car. Luckily, the driver saw me, stopped and rushed me to the nearest hospital.

Much later, they caught the hitchhikers who tried to murder me. Sadly, it was only after they had killed a little boy in Arizona. They were extradited to Florida so I could identify them. I'm sure they were surprised to find me still alive. But you know, I don't think I would have lived if they hadn't gotten my car stuck in the mud. Laughing at that is what enabled me to survive.

As a matter of fact, laughter helps me to this day. When I went back to work, people did not know how to act around me, so I started making jokes. I told them since I got stabbed 16 times, I went from being 'Chris' to 'Swiss.' That line always brings a laugh. When people started feeling more comfortable with what happened to me, they started giving me nicknames like 'Slash' or 'Stick.' I laugh every time they call me something like that. Why shouldn't I? Laughing is why I am still here."

HUMOR IN THE HOLOCAUST

Jack Mandlebaum is a Holocaust survivor. When Jack was 12 years old, the Nazis invaded Poland and Jack's family relocated to the Polish town of Dzialoszyce. His father was captured during a "cleansing aktion" on September 14, 1939, deported to Stutthoff Concentration Camp and murdered. Jack was captured at age 13 in his mother's home town of Slawkow and worked in a series of forced labor camps over the next two years.

In June of 1942, 15-year-old Mandlebaum was separated from his mother and younger brother, transferred to Blechammer Concentration Camp and assigned prisoner number 16013. Blechammer would be only one of the many concentration camps where Jack Mandlebaum would spend his teenage years.

On May 7, 1945 the Russian Army liberated Jack from Derhau Concentration Camp and he found every member of his family had been killed in the gas chambers of Auschwitz. It was not until June 24, 1946 when Jack Mandlebaum arrived in the United States to begin a new life.

"We would laugh at the guards behind their back," Jack said.

Jack says his experience was nothing like the Academy Award-winning movie "Life is Beautiful."

"That movie," he says smiling wryly, "was a nice fable — but impossible. We could never laugh in front of the guards. But if we had any opportunity to laugh away from them, we would take it. It was always after the fact, when we knew we were not being watched or listened to.

We would make fun of some of the guards' physical types. There was one guard who had a short leg. We would mimic him, but only when we were alone — at night maybe. Thinking back and laughing about what we had seen or heard made it a little easier to get through a day."

Jack continues, "My partner and friend was named Moniek. You needed to pair up to survive. You could get strength from your other half. Moniek and I were assigned as cooks for the guards. Working in the kitchen, we managed to stay strong because we would eat more. We would also steal food for other prisoners, to help them live, too. Each prisoner was given only 600 calories of food a day but needed 5000 just to do the work they demanded. We absolutely could not live on the food given to us, so we had to steal.

Once, Moniek and I were asked to clean out a food locker. The floor was made of black slate, so the water in the pail would turn black as we cleaned. That is how we stole margarine. We would cover the margarine in dirty rags, hiding it in the black water. We got three pounds of margarine that way. We took risks to survive — and help others do the same. At the end of the day, we would laugh at how we tricked them.

Our camp did not have a crematorium for the dead bodies, so Moniek and I had to haul and stack bodies onto a truck. The bodies we stacked were of fellow Jews we had seen and known. We would laugh and make jokes about the bodies — the weird or funny positions they were in. It was our distraction. I often wondered who was going to be throwing me off someday.

We would also make bets on how long people would last. That was another way we used humor as a distraction of what was happening around us.

To survive, you had to find a way to see the humor. Those who did, made it easier on themselves. Every morning, I would make myself think, 'Today I am going to have a great day.'"

Jack concludes, "Time and reflection are no friend to the Holocaust survivor. I don't want to dwell on the things that happened to me, so I find joy in my friends and family every day."

Chapter Nine

You Just Have to Laugh ... at Funerals

"One joy scatters a hundred griefs."
— Chinese Proverb

The gift of humor is like the gift of faith. Both have the power to lift us above the pain of life, and let us see the goodness and joy all around.

Rabbi Alan Cohen explains:

"Laughter is important in grief. A member of my congregation told me about a woman in her 60s who was dying of cancer. Her doctor came into her hospital room for her morning examination. The dying woman looked up at the doctor before starting her check-up and said, 'You are going to touch me in some very intimate places. I sure hope your hands are warm.'"

The Rabbi continues, "The most terminally ill person wants to laugh. They don't want to spend their entire day crying and feeling sorrow. So, when I go to visit them, I will make a funny comment on an honest moment or situation.

I use that same approach when giving a eulogy. I'll take a real and honest trait of the dearly departed and bring joy in their memory. One time, the man I was eulogizing was known for being perpetually late. At the service I said, 'Today, finally he was on time.' Another time, I said of a woman, 'She would never ever let me get the last word. Today, I will.'

I've made comments about people being a bad cook or even that this one could never get the color of his socks to match. I don't make these comments to be known as a funny guy, I choose my words carefully to evoke a pleasant memory of the dearly departed. The people in attendance and especially the family always appreciate those funny memories. Laughter is a celebration of life, so bringing joy to a grieving family about their lost loved one is the perfect gift."

WILE E. COYOTE

The following person wished to remain anonymous:

"When my father died four years ago, it was a difficult time for everyone in our family. It was especially hard on my mother, who nearly died a year before from a genetic blood disorder. I firmly believe my somewhat sick sense of humor helped us get through the hardest times.

After dad's death, the entire family was at the funeral home making arrangements for the service. The funeral director asked what type of music my father liked. Before I could stop myself, I blurted out, 'In-a-godda-da-vida' by Iron Butterfly. What else could I say? It was my dad's favorite song, and he would have loved the idea of having it played at his funeral.

One of dad's greatest passions was building model airplanes. The first plane he ever built was called 'Wiley.' Wiley was a yellow and orange, single prop plane. Dad found a flexible Wile E. Coyote toy, which he stuck in the cockpit of the plane. My father then put tiny goggles and a little scarf around Wiley's neck, turned the toy's head slightly, and bent up the middle finger on one hand. With that wonderful grin on Wiley's face, it was a hilarious sight. Even after 'Wiley' crashed, dad kept the wrecked plane in the shed for years, just in case he ever wanted to repair it.

While planning the funeral service, my sister and I decided to make a collage of my father to be displayed at the memorial. We wanted the collage to include photographs of dad when he was a child, through his Air Force days and motorcycle races, right up to the very last photo taken of him.

This final photograph was of dad and mom sitting on our back porch. In the picture, my father is sitting in a chair watering the lawn, but he is holding the hose between his legs, making it look like he was ... well, I think you get the idea. I really had to fight other family members to let us put that picture in the collage. Many felt it was inappropriate, but I insisted that the snapshot epitomized my dad's sense of humor. After the service, mom and I were sitting in a pew. She was distraught. With tears rolling down her cheeks, she said, 'At least no one said anything about the 'garden hose' picture.'

I told her I was more worried about the 'Wiley picture.'

Remembering 'Wiley's' raised middle finger, mom suddenly laughed. That's when I knew she would be okay."

LIFETIME GUARANTEE

Martha Blazek says, "A good laugh goes a long way. Last summer a family member named Ken found out he had terminal brain cancer. Ken was given three to six months to live. We took the steps needed to make a smooth transition — getting a lawyer, making a will, selling the house and planning the funeral.

Sadly, Ken died earlier than anticipated. We flew to be with his family at this sad and difficult time. The funeral home called and said the body was ready to be viewed. Diane, Ken's wife, who had been a pillar of strength, asked us to go with her to the funeral home because she was unsure of how she would react.

Before they viewed Ken's body, the funeral director explained to Diane that, because Ken died before the casket they ordered had arrived, the casket being used was not the one she and Ken originally selected. Using his most empathetic and somber voice, the funeral director assured Diane that the casket being used was an upgraded model with 'highly distinctive features.' He also said that the manufacturer of the casket would be planting a tree in Ken's name, but the family would never know what type of tree, where it was planted and there would be no marker identifying it with Ken.

We all started looking at each other, obviously thinking, 'Why even tell us then?' The fact that we would never know the kind of tree, where it was and there would be no marker made the whole thing seem ridiculously funny.

The director then added that Diane would receive a letter in the mail containing a lifetime guarantee for the casket. We looked at each other, mouthing the words: 'What is he talking about?' and 'Who's lifetime?'

Using his soft, solemn voice, the funeral director continued to explain the details of the burial ceremony. All the while, we were trying to contain our laughter, wondering who would dig up a casket to see if the 'lifetime warranty' was good."

"As long as the casket makes it in the ground," Martha concludes, "who really cares about some 'lifetime guarantee'? It may seem silly, but that moment helped all of us — especially Diane — deal with a very difficult time."

A MOUNTAIN OF LAUGHTER

Kim Shaffer recounts her family's ability to laugh during two separate funerals.

"My grandmother had a mastectomy in June of 1980. It was a very long and painful five-and-a-half years before she passed away. When my sister and I went to see grandma at the funeral home, it was all we could do to keep from laughing out loud.

You see, one of grandma's breasts was obviously much larger than the other. It was a mountain next to a valley. Just as we were noticing this, a friend walked up, stood next to us and said, 'Doesn't she look beautiful?'

That's all it took. My sister and I burst out laughing. The woman was shocked, but my sister and I later agreed that grandma was probably laughing the hardest."

Kim's brother-in-law, Mike Smith, had three open-heart surgeries. Despite these troubles, Mike was very outgoing and full of life. He was always talking in his loud, booming voice and loved to laugh.

Finally, Mike's heart could hold out no longer. At the funeral home, everyone was very sad and extremely quiet. Then one of Mike's best friends, Kyle, walked in the visitation room. He looked around. Then, deliberately speaking loudly — so everyone could hear, Kyle blurted out, "You know, this is the quietest I have ever heard Mike!"

"Everyone laughed," Kim concludes. "That was the moment the healing began."

TIME ZONED

Barbara Johnson explains:

"My brother-in-law unexpectedly died in March. During his funeral, people were invited to share memories of him. I got up and told this favorite story. It took place about a week before he died.

It was college basketball season. Now, I live on the West Coast and always seem confused about how TV broadcasters handle the three-hour time difference. I asked my brother-in-law if the games were delayed or broadcast at the same time or what. He thought it was hilarious that I couldn't grasp the nuances of different time zones.

So, one Saturday I called anxiously because I knew he would be watching the Wake Forest/Duke game, and I was desperate to get the score. As a rabid Wake fan, I was disturbed to hear that the Demon Deacons were losing decisively.

My brother-in-law consoled me by saying, 'There is still hope.' 'What do you mean?' I asked, thinking my team might have a comeback left in them.

My brother-in-law told me, 'Well, where you are the game hasn't started yet. So maybe Wake will do better.'

That story brought down the house at the funeral and cheered everyone up. Especially me."

HEAVENLY GREETERS

Lori Williams-Horn discovered how, during times of great loss and tragedy, even a little bit of humor can do wonders. Here are Lori's words:

"Eight years ago, my cousin's 13-year-old son, Danny, was tragically killed while roller-blading. Following the accident, the family met at my cousin's house and all began crying and talking. My father and I began talking about what a wonderful person Danny was.

Then I said, 'Hey, I wonder if when people die, there would be a large display in heaven, like the type they have in airports to show the daily arrivals? The loved ones who have gone before would say, 'Look who is coming in today ... let's go meet them!'

At this thought, my father and I began to laugh. For the next few days, we would look at each other and smile, thinking of this 'Great Concourse in the Sky.' Granted, this is not a knee-slapper, but it really made it easier to deal with the loss of a wonderful young man."

HUMOR MATTERS

Steve Sultanoff, Ph.D. describes himself as a recovering "serious person" and a clinical Mirthologist by trade. One of his earliest lessons in the healing power of humor came when he was 17 and his father died of a heart attack.

"After dad's funeral," says Dr. Steve, "many friends and relatives gathered in my home, including my high school French teacher. My teacher was cheerful, and shared stories that lightened the somber atmosphere. Many of us even laughed out loud.

Later, I overheard some of my mother's friends criticizing this teacher's behavior as being irreverent and disrespectful. I really did not agree. My teacher telling stories did not diminish the pain that I felt at my father's death, but it sure did lessen my suffering. In those humorous moments, the heavy, somber atmosphere was lightened, and I felt a great sense of relief.

I still believe to this day that dealing with my father's death was easier because I laughed. My teacher's use of humor showed me that life continues. Laughter served as a great gift in a time of enormous distress."

WHOOPEE!

Jo-Anne Brown lost a loved one, but still found a way to laugh:

"After a death in the family, we were all understandably upset. The evening after the funeral, my husband and I were invited to the home of the deceased.

My husband brought a device called a 'Redi-Poot' along with him. A Redi-Poot is a hand-held whoopee cushion which sounds just like the real thing. Even though my husband had this device for over a year, for some reason he decided this was the night to use it.

We informed the deceased's family that we had brought the device, and also got their permission to use it. Believe it or not, that Redi-Poot was a godsend that night.

When someone opened the refrigerator, my husband would let it rip. When a woman bent over to pick up her baby, he let 'er rip again. People actually thought my husband was breaking wind! One lady got up and moved away from him. Another woman insisted that the smell was appalling. This went on all night. The expressions on people's faces were priceless.

As people were leaving, we let them in on the joke so they wouldn't think my husband was a complete pig. We thought everyone was in on the prank, but we were wrong. It turned out we had left out one very important person.

It seems Lisa, the daughter of the deceased, had stayed in her room all night because she was so disgusted by the Redi-Poot sound. Every time Lisa came out to join the family, she heard another rip and immediately retreated to her room. Then, after all of the guests had left, Lisa asked her dad, 'What is wrong with Uncle Pug (my husband)?'

When her dad called us the next day and told us what Lisa had said, it cracked us up even more. Then, I immediately called Lisa to apologize.

Once I explained what Uncle Pug had done, she wasn't upset at all. As a matter of fact, she told me, 'It was good to hear laughter.' Then adding, 'After mom died, I never thought I would hear my dad or sister laugh again. Thanks.'"

WRONG LINE

Scott Beeler was 14 when he made his first visit to a funeral home. His best friend's younger brother died and — to pay their respects — Scott went to view the body with another pal, Russ.

Scott begins, "It was my first funeral home experience and I was pretty nervous about it. The line was real long to view the body and somehow Russ and I got separated. I watched as he got closer to the open casket. Then I saw him cover his mouth, like he was holding in laughter, and run from the room.

Now I was getting closer to the boy's casket and getting scared, thinking about seeing my first dead body — let alone that of somebody I knew. As I got closer, I saw what Russ saw — and why he was holding in his laughter.

In the casket was an old lady. We had gotten the wrong viewing room, hence were in the wrong line. We barely made it out of the funeral home before we started breaking up with laughter. We weren't laughing out of disrespect for the deceased, more out of our own nervousness and discomfort — and the silliness of what we had done.

To this day — 32 years later — every time I have to attend a funeral, I think of that story. It still makes me laugh, relaxing me in the face of a sad situation."

TIGER

Bob Goldhammer was a paramedic from 1974 through 1998. During that time, he saw a lot of sad situations, and a lot of situations which were downright funny. He also cared for a lot of people with terminal diseases, but none of his experiences prepared him for the news that his wife had inflammatory breast cancer.

"This particular type of cancer," Bob says, "is rapid onset and always terminal within a short period of time. But, despite the multiple surgeries, radiation, chemotherapy treatments and blood transfusions, my wife never lost her sense of humor. When we were told that there was no more the doctors could do and she was to receive her last blood transfusion, she laughed and said, 'I'm like the tiger in those old Exxon commercials. I'm getting my last fill-up.'

On the morning of her funeral, I gathered a few mementos to place in her casket. There were pictures of our four boys, a bottle of her favorite perfume, some drawings and a few other meaningful items. The last thing I added was her airline frequent flyer card. I told her, 'You might as well get credit for the trip you're about to go on, because I'm guessing you're about to rack up a lot of miles.'

My wife always told me that laughing and keeping a sense of humor will help you through anything. She was right."

LAUGHING WITH THE WORLD

The following poem was written by Amy L. Fridrich, an occupational therapy nurse. One of her terminally ill patients had taken a turn for the worse. This was a very special man, she says, who always had a smile for others, always reminded everyone to be thankful for each and every day and truly understood the importance of humor.

After the patient's passing, she wrote this poem.

Laughing With the World

Emotions of laughter dance among shared memories,
Darkened only by the looming of an aged body drifting further away.
I am witness to time fading ever so slowly, yet still too fast, at least for me.
My heavy heart is quickly lightened as a smile evolves past his wrinkled layers,
Gently masking the ever-present pain.

His eyes gently close.
The repetition of labored breathing allows my mind to wander as I carefully examine every work-hardened line on his embraced hand.

I can read stories in the misformed knuckles and imagine the pain, pain that was never expressed.

So many thoughts drown in my mind,
yet I am unable to determine the words to express how I feel.
Silence prevails, and I struggle, knowing regret will surely follow.
Abruptly, my thoughts are ceased by his tightened grasp and my undivided attention stares into his clear blue eyes.

My hand gently brushes across his whitened brow.
Hoping a simple touch will restore the tanned complexion he always shone.
Yet, it is he not I, who finds the words to speak.
Revealing wisdom of his years, he whispers, "Laughter is God's song, Universal in it's being, it brings us happiness.
Just remember to always keep laughing with the world."

Chapter Ten

You Just Have To Laugh ... in the Hospital

"Laughter is the relief, the tonic, the surcease for pain!"
— Charles Chaplin

Hospital stays can be an awful lot of fun, can't they? Consider the wonderful amenities: highly trained medical professionals at your beck and call, cable TV, a bed that moves, lots of nice drugs. Heck, you don't even need to get up to use the bathroom, as the convenience of catheters and bedpans make such troublesome trips utterly unnecessary. All this, plus fabulous gourmet cuisine delivered directly to your luxurious suite, 24 hours a day. What more could anyone want?

Okay, let's face it. Being in the hospital sucks. You are there because you are sick. If you want to get well, your medical team has to do their job, but you have to do yours as well. What is your job? Keeping your spirits high. How do you do it? Well, after reading this far, you really ought to know. If you answered,

"Humor and laughing," you may move on and read the stories below. If you answered, "By getting angry and throwing things at the night nurse," please go back and re-read this book from the beginning.

The following people managed to make the hospital just a little bit more fun. Please enjoy their stories.

ARE YOU WITH ME DOCTOR WU?

Weekend warrior second baseman Richard Stern was turning the pivot on a routine double play in his summer city baseball league. Taking the throw from shortstop, he wheeled, whipping the ball to first base. The base runner came charging at Richard like a freight train and threw a cross-body block, snapping Richard's leg in half from the knee down. Richard lay on the ground in excruciating pain.

In the emergency room, Richard says, "The attendant on duty asked me who my doctor was.

'Dr. Wu,' I said.

The attendant asked, 'Who?'

I repeated, 'Wu! The doctor's name is Wu!'"

"It was beginning," Richard said, "to sound like a bad imitation of the 'Who's on First?' Abbott and Costello routine."

With the help of the yellow pages, Richard finally communicated the doctor's name. The comedy continued, though, when the resident doctor walked in and was — for some unexplained reason — dressed like a cowboy. His first words to Richard were, "Did you get shot?" Richard shook his head grinning and said, "No way buck-a-roo." The doctor shrugged and proceeded to prep Richard for surgery.

Afterwards, ol' Doc Holliday put Richard's leg in a cast and told him they would have to reset the leg in three weeks.

"That won't work," Richard said, "I'm too busy at work." Richard was worried that a lack of mobility would seriously damage his career in the fast-paced, highly competitive world of advertising. He was right.

Five weeks passed and Richard was becoming severely depressed. First of all, he was not working and his career was suffering. Even knowing that he recently won a 'Cleo' award for excellence in advertising didn't cheer him up. He was literally going from the top of his profession to becoming a nobody. He had no money coming in and had only $400 left in his bank account. Furthermore, he was completely dependent on other people which made him feel helpless, vulnerable and weak. Finally, and most disturbingly, his leg was not healing properly at all.

"I thought of suicide, but since my medication was only given to me a few pills at a time, I couldn't swallow a whole bottle," Richard said. "I wanted to put my head in a gas oven. Believe me, if I could have made it to the stove, I would have. I had hit rock bottom.

For whatever reason, I started thinking of my grandpa. I remembered what a jokester and fun person he was. I knew that if grandpa was still alive, he would not have felt sorry for me and would never let me feel sorry for myself.

Thinking about grandpa, I decided it was time to start laughing — at everything. I *made* myself laugh. I began reflecting on my accident. From the 'Wu is the doctor?' routine in the ER, to the cowpoke surgeon, I began to see the ridiculousness of it all. I made a conscious decision to find something funny in everything and laugh."

The change was remarkable. During Richard's weeks of depression, his bones had shown virtually no sign of growth or healing. Three weeks into his new found, funny mind set, however, he went in for another X-ray. Afterwards, the doctor came out and asked, "What the hell have you been doing? Your healing has progressed 35%!"

Richard concluded that instead of depression controlling him, he would take control of it. "It wasn't easy," he says. "It was a moment-to-moment struggle. I figured the more humorous moments I can string together, the more my new perspective would take hold. Negativity eats at the soul. The only thing I found to replenish and nourish my soul was laughing. In a way, the most motivating factor in my life was going through that negativity, because now I have found the value and magic of laughing — and I am never going to let it go."

THANK YOU DR. WILLIAMS

Everyone knows actor Christopher Reeve suffered a tragic accident which left him paralyzed from the neck down. What some may not know is how the gift of laughter brought light to one of his darkest moments.

The first week in the hospital, while lying in traction, Christopher realized he may never walk again. As he lay upside-down in traction, he had thoughts of ending his life, thinking that it was pointless to go on.

Just as he was sinking into this deep despair, he heard a lot of commotion. There seemed to be a doctor in the room making a lot of noise and talking in a very unusual accent.

Just then Christopher's traction table was flipped over so he was suddenly face-up, looking directly at his good buddy, Robin Williams.

Robin was doing a hysterical impression of a Russian doctor. In his thick, silly accent Robin said, "I understand you're paralyzed in vun position. Dat vouldn't be the position I vould have chosen." Christopher smiled some. Robin kept the lines coming with his typical, manic intensity. Finally, Christopher laughed out loud. He then looked over and saw his wife laughing, too, holding their child.

That moment shocked him out of his depression. At that instant, he realized he had a lot to live for — the most important things anyone can have: family and friends.

THE GREAT PIZZA CAPER

While in college, 20-year-old Nan Marr contracted Addison's Disease. She lost all mobility in her legs and her adrenal glands quit working. The disease then moved upwards, immobilizing her from her neck down. Nan was told by a specialist she would never walk again.

"I figured I had a couple of choices," Nan said. "The first was to drown in self-pity. The second was to try and find the humor. I went for the laughs.

My first roommate in the hospital helped set the tone. Even though she had no legs, was paralyzed, had no hair and soaked her teeth in a jar, she was a hoot. When I first walked in the room I saw her in bed and asked how she felt. She said, laughing, 'How would I know? I'm paralyzed. I can't 'feel' a thing!'"

"My parents," Nan continues, "helped me keep it fun. They would smuggle soda pop and snacks into my room because the hospital food was bad. The food was so bad, in fact, some of the patients on my floor decided we had to have some pizza. Of course, the hospital had set strict diets for us, but we didn't care. We wanted pizza! It was time for an act of rebellion. Since the nurses would never agree to let us have some pie, we had to work in secret and as a team.

We distracted the nurses while one paralyzed guy dialed the pizza shop by using a pencil held in his mouth. Next, we assembled a team to secretly meet the delivery man downstairs.

The 'Pizza Team' included me, who was in a wheelchair; Bob, who was also confined to a wheelchair; and Mary Ann, a dwarf with stubs for legs who was also paraplegic, and had to lay stomach down on a gurney to move. Our final team member was Jeff, the victim of a gunshot wound, stuck in a wheelchair and paralyzed from the waist down.

It was a 30-minute delivery — and it took us all that time just to sneak downstairs! We helped each other get to the service elevators, hold open the doors and get inside. It wasn't easy to be quiet and keep hidden from the staff, but we managed to do it.

When the pizza man arrived, he looked in the window where we had said to meet us. Since we were all in wheelchairs and a gurney, we were too low and he couldn't see us! Finally, he spotted us and we opened the door for him. I told the pizza man to put all six pizzas on my lap. He said they were too hot to put on my legs. I laughed, explaining I was paralyzed from the waist down! I wouldn't be able to feel any temperature. The delivery man took the money out of my purse, left the change and went on his way.

Then we snuck to the occupational therapy room to munch some pizza. We helped each other eat, and someone even invented a tool so we could open the soda cans. Once we had eaten our fill, we decided to share the rest with the other patients on our floor.

Now we had the task of getting everybody back upstairs. It was difficult enough before, but now we had the pizzas and sodas to contend with. Our plan was working though. We thought we were home free, and were all getting excited about the prospect of bringing some pizza to our friends. Then the elevator doors opened and a bunch of nurses were standing there, scowling at us with folded arms. They immediately confiscated our pizza and sodas. In fact, they really seemed to enjoy catching us. One started scolding us like we were children, barking out, 'You are all grounded!' We laughed.

I said, 'Grounded? We're all paralyzed! Where do you think we are going?'

They took us back to our rooms and made sure no one else got any pizza or pop. One nurse even called my dad to tell him what I had done. Dad responded, 'Good for her.'

It was that kind of persistence and light-heartedness that kept me going. When the doctor told me I would never walk again, I laughed at him. I would stay in physical therapy for hours and hours. I was always falling down, but I wasn't going to quit. One time, someone found me on the floor after-hours because I had fallen and no one was around. They helped me up. I just laughed at myself and got back to work. I was determined to walk again."

Today, years later, Nan Marr is walking. "When part of your life has been taken away," Nan says, "you have to love each day. I make sure if I ever get down, I look in the mirror and think, 'I'm standing and walking today because of determination and a lot of laughing.' If I didn't find the humor in things, I would still be in a wheelchair. If you can't laugh, you give up."

WE'RE ALL NUTS

Everyone loved Mary. She was always upbeat, funny, outrageous and appeared to have it all together. She was a workaholic, outspoken, always first in any line and a pillar of strength to anybody who worked with her. No one at the home savings business where she worked knew that she would soon be diagnosed with bi-polar and manic-depressive disorders.

When the Federal Trade Commission attempted to shut down her employer, stress began to rear its ugly head around the office. One woman at the company got a palsy, one guy got the shingles, another started having heart problems.

Mary says, "One day, it all got to me. I guess it was all building up. I began to hyperventilate, then I collapsed. As the ambulance drivers were wheeling me through the office, I asked them to pull the sheet over my head. I just couldn't bear the thought of 150 fellow employees watching me get hauled off by paramedics. I would rather have had them think I was dead than think that I couldn't handle the pressure of our failing business."

Mary continues, "When they told me I was going to the mental ward, I cringed thinking of 'One Flew Over the Cuckoos Nest.' Deep inside, though, I knew I needed to be there.

There was one patient in the mental hospital who gave me a one-liner that put it all together for me and got me back on the right track. I still laugh out loud every time I think about it. We were eating lunch in the cafeteria, talking about our problems, when this fellow just looked at me and said, 'Listen, you're nuts. I'm nuts. Everybody is nuts. We just got caught.'"

RUPTURED WITH LAUGHTER

In 1967, Walter Bemak ruptured a disk in his lower back and was paralyzed from the waist down. The doctors removed the disk, but decided to wait two weeks before doing a fusion to see if he might get some nerve regeneration.

Walter says, "That left me lying flat on my back in bed, unable to go anywhere, and under strict orders not to move under any circumstances. I also was blessed with the unbridled joy that is a catheter.

One night, being heavily medicated, I was hallucinating that I had been captured by the Germans during WWII and was being transported in a truck. In the hallucination, I was trying to climb over the wooden barriers on the side of the truck. What I was really doing, though, was climbing over the guardrail of my hospital bed. At some point, I woke up lying on the floor.

Now, my roommate was an 82-year-old man who had a broken neck and was lying in bed with his head immobilized. So now picture the scene: I'm lying on the floor with all kinds of tubes sticking out of me, paralyzed from the waist down, yelling for help from a guy who can't even move his head. He finally does manage to yell into the intercom, and I soon heard feet coming down the hall. A nurse came into the room. I could hear another set of feet running down the hall behind her.

So, the nurse is looking at me lying there, in desperate need of medical attention. I could have damaged my bladder, my penis, or done even more harm to my ailing back, and the very first thing she does is shout to the person behind her. And what does she shout? Is it 'I need help!' 'Code Blue!' or any of that other ER jargon? Nope, she calls out, 'Don't anybody come in! He's naked!'

Tell me humor can't help people through their pain."

A RASH REACTION

Amy begins, "Seven years ago, my daughter and mother were the only ones in the house. I was curling my hair when I heard a crash and my mother screaming out my name. With all kinds of wild scenarios flashing through my head, I ran up the stairs to see what happened. I found my mother lying on the bed with a red rash visibly moving up her body. Mom said she was having an allergic reaction and needed to get to an emergency room. I was so scared, I didn't think I would be able to drive her to the hospital, so I called 911.

After we arrived at the hospital, I would not leave my mother's side. I remember clutching my three-year-old while watching my mother's body shake violently. Just then, a male nurse entered the room, took one look at my mother and said, 'You didn't have to try and kill yourself to see me. You could have called.'

My jaw hit the floor, but it was my mother's reaction that shocked me even more. She smiled at the nurse, then began laughing. It turned out she had worked with this nurse 13 years before — in the very same hospital. As the doctor administered the appropriate medication, the nurse continued to make mom laugh by telling funny stories. It kept her mind occupied, while we waited for the drugs to kick in."

B.V. (BEFORE VIAGRA)

Dixie Peterson appreciates how laughter can help during a really hard time.

"My friend, Becky, had just had a baby," Dixie says. "Another friend, Christie, and I went to visit Becky in the maternity ward. While we were there, Julie, an acquaintance from our church, came into the room. I asked what brought her to the hospital.

Lowering her chin to her chest and looking down at the floor she said, 'Richard, my husband, is in this hospital. He is in a room on this floor actually. He ... um ... has an erection that won't go down. It's a reaction from his heart medicines.' We didn't know what to say except, 'Oh.' We were quite honestly shocked she would even tell us about her husband's unusual condition. Then, as soon as she left the room, we immediately broke into hysterical laughter. We started making jokes — wanting to know if we could get the same medication so we could slip it into our husbands' mashed potatoes. We continued laughing while imagining what we would say if we went into the poor man's room. Things like: 'Oh, I see you have a tent in your bed,' and 'How 'long' have you been here?' ... 'What's 'up'?' ... 'I bet it's 'hard' lying in that bed all day.'

With each of these comments we laughed harder and louder. Becky even begged us to shut up because her stitches hurt from laughing so much. Ignoring her, we decided a good gift for someone with that particular problem would be a ring toss game. Just then Julie came back in the room and told us that Richard would like us to come visit. 'Oh no,' I thought.

Well, we went into his room, but were very careful not to let our eyes wander. We knew if we looked at the area of Richard's condition or at each other in the eye, we would lose it and laugh. To this day, none of us can remember what was said in that room, just that we did everything we could to keep ourselves composed.

As the years have passed, Becky, Christy and I still laugh about Richard's unusual problem. One time, I got a ring toss game in the mail with no note attached. I laughed all day over that package. Every time any one of us retells the story, it brings laughter. The latest funny comment was when an older woman I told the story to laughed and said, 'I guess people wouldn't call that Richard 'Dick' for short.'"

Chapter Eleven

You Just Have To Laugh ... at the Last Chapter

"Life is too important to be taken seriously!"
— Oscar Wilde

So here we go ... the final chapter. This is where I put it all together — The Big Finish, as we say in the comedy biz.

I have done my best to show you that laughter can help you through life's biggest obstacles. There are other folks who not only support that statement but have studied the physical benefits of laughter as well.

Dr. Michael Miller is the Director for the Center of Preventive Cardiology at the University of Maryland Medical Center. Dr. Miller states:

"The old saying that 'laughter is the best medicine,' definitely appears to be true when it comes to protecting your heart. We know that mental stress is associated with impairment of the endothelium, the protective barrier lining our blood vessels. This can cause a series of inflammatory reactions that lead to fat and cholesterol build-up in the coronary arteries imately, to a heart attack.

Laughter, along with an active sense of humor, may help protect you against a heart attack. People with heart disease are less likely to recognize humor or use it to get out of uncomfortable situations. They generally laughed less, even in positive situations, and they displayed more anger and hostility.

The ability to laugh — either naturally or as a learned behavior — may have important implications in societies such as the U.S., where heart disease remains the number one killer."

Dr. Miller concludes, "We know that exercising, not smoking and eating foods low in saturated fat will reduce the risk of heart disease. Perhaps regular, hearty laughter should be added to the list."

Dr. William Fry, a professor of psychiatry at Stanford Medical School, has spent more than 40 years studying the physical effects of laughter.

"Laughing has an immediate impact on the body," he says. "The brain is stimulated into greater alertness, enhancing memory and sociability."

Dr. Fry adds that laughter increases the concentration of antibodies circulating in the blood stream, thus strengthening our immune system. This means a person who laughs a lot is more resistant to developing infection and other illnesses.

The New England Journal of Medicine also supports the physical benefits of laughing. In the 1980 article, Dr. Franz Ingelfinger estimated that 85% of all human illnesses can be cured by systems already present in our bodies. For example, there is a healing agent called Immunoglobulin A or IgA. These IgAs are produced by our immune system and are the body's first line of defense. They attack foreign organisms, protect us from respiratory problems and can even destroy tumor cells and viruses. What is really amazing is that the presence of IgA will rise and fall in accordance with our mood. People with a well-developed sense of humor have been proven to have increased concentrations of IgA in their bodies!

So, we all just have to laugh because it's good for our health. Now add to that my research, this book and it's easy to understand why laughing is not only emotionally healthy, it is absolutely imperative to ease us through the really tough times.

I am not suggesting it's wrong to get sad, frustrated and angry when life blind sides us, but for goodness sakes, why let fear, anxiety and worry pollute our daily existence? All the worrying in the world won't make anyone's life one bit longer. In fact, the stress of too much worry will probably shave off a few days, months or even years.

Don't think that good, clean living will prevent any bad things from happening, either. You can be a God-fearing person, follow the Golden Rule and call your parents every single night. You can work 14-hour days providing for your family, build houses for the homeless all weekend and spend your free time volunteering at a children's hospital. You can even sell all your worldly possessions, move to Calcutta and continue the work of Mother Teresa. It doesn't make any difference. No matter how good of a person you are, illness, injury and death will come.

So what? Like my buddies said while serving in Vietnam, "Ain't no big thing. Don't mean nothing." We all have to laugh, and find humor in every curve ball life throws at us.

Remember how Ginny Klempnauer — battered and bloody by a terrible car accident — responded to the paramedic who asked her height, weight and age? Ginny replied, "Somebody slap him. You don't ask a lady her weight and age."

The paramedic said, "Oh boy, we've got a live one here."

Ginny said, "Yes you do — and let's keep it that way!"

Recall how "sit-down" comedian Paul Shryack made the choice to laugh at having Cerebral Palsy. He even invites his audiences to laugh at it as well:

"How many CP guys does it take to screw in a light bulb?" Paul asks, then waits. "One ... but it takes 100 bulbs."

Remember Bob Rowlands as he lay in his bed, hours before his passing. He drank non-alcoholic beer through a straw and cracked jokes with his family.

"Before you pull the sheet over me, make sure I'm dead," Bob said. "And when you cremate me, make sure I don't have a pulse before you stick me in there."

In the very first chapter of this book, at the very top of the very first page is a quote from George Bernard Shaw. As a matter of fact, I am a bit envious of Mr. Shaw. He was able to put in one sentence what took me an entire book to prove. Please do me the favor of reading his words one more time. It ties a neat and pretty little bow around the premise of this book.

"Life does not cease to be funny when something bad happens any more than it ceases to be serious when we are laughing."

Ain't that the truth!

P.S. I fibbed a little bit. There is actually one more chapter in the book — a really fun one, too. Keep reading and ...

KEEP LAUGHING!

Chapter Twelve

You Just Have To Laugh ... at the Very Last Chapter of This Book *(I really mean it this time!)*

This chapter is filled with games, quizzes and puzzles based on the stories you have just read. Play these games by yourself, with family or with a sick friend. (Quick Tip: If you play with someone who hasn't read the book, or is dead, you will almost certainly win.)

The reader with the most correct answers might be a grand prize winner of One Million Dollars!!! Not from me, of course, but from the lottery of your choice — if you happen to pick the correct numbers, and the prize is that high. (Lottery tickets not included. Not applicable in any of the 50 states, any other country, planet or galaxy. Taxes and surcharges may apply. Some assembly required. No right turn on red.)

Warning: These games offer a humorous perspective on some pretty serious issues. In case you have forgotten, that's the premise, babe!

MULTIPLE CHOICE

Choose the correct answer from the choices listed:

1) The three obstacles people laugh at in this book:
   A. Illness, Injury and Death
   B. The IRS, the FTC and the M.O.B.
   C. Bad Breath, Body Odor and Waxy Yellow Build-up

2) This book refers to laughter as ...
   A. The Gift Of Laughter
   B. Laughter is the Perfect Gift
   C. Gift, Schmift ... I want cold, hard cash

3) Laughter is the _______ that will offer shelter during life's stormy times.
   A. Umbrella
   B. Lifeboat
   C. Stormy times? What stormy times? My life has never been anything but sheer perfection.

4) According to Uncle Lou, how many animals could Old MacDonald have on his farm?
   A. As many as there was on Noah's Ark
   B. 187,491
   C. As many as he damn well wants

5) What were Johnny and Bob Rowlands wearing while wheeling through their living room?
   A. Daffy Duck pajamas
   B. Matching lime green leisure suits
   C. Nothing but skin and smiles

6) Policewoman Pat Rogers wore something on her necklace to diffuse tension. Was it:
   - A. A pig charm
   - B. A handcuff charm
   - C. Lucky Charms

7) To ease the unease created by her Alzheimer's, Grandma Kiki would sing:
   - A. Arias from her favorite operas
   - B. Broadway show tunes
   - C. "Play That Funky Music White Boy"

8) The U.S. Senator who laughed on national television after losing a bid for the Presidency:
   - A. John Quincy Adams
   - B. Bob Dole
   - C. Senator John Blutowski

9) What was the Jones Field air traffic controller's response to a pilot who called over the radio: "Jones Field, guess who?"
   - A. "Um ... Amelia Earhart?"
   - B. "Someone who doesn't use proper communications terminology?"
   - C. "Guess where?" and turned off the airport lights

10) Two 14-year-old boys began laughing in a funeral home because:
   - A. They told each other a joke
   - B. They were pallbearers and dropped the coffin
   - C. They were at the wrong funeral

11) Martha Blazek and family members almost broke out in hysterics when the funeral director told the family the casket came with:
    A. Air conditioning
    B. A lifetime guarantee
    C. All-weather siding

12) Uncle Pug got family and friends laughing after a funeral service by using:
    A. A red clown nose
    B. A Redi-Poot whoopee cushion
    C. Nothing. Uncle Pug was the deceased.

13) After a tornado ripped through a farm in central Kansas, Rags Smith discovered a friend sitting in a trailer. What did her friend say?
    A. "I've got to use the bathroom!"
    B. "Might as well eat pie!"
    C. "There's no place like home. There's no place like home."

14) After falling to the floor of his hospital room, the nurse who found Walter Bemak said:
    A. "Yoga class isn't for two more hours."
    B. "Don't anybody come in! He's naked!"
    C. "Will you clean under the bed so I won't have to?"

15) When Linda Ellerbee lost her hair to chemotherapy, her daughter told her she looked like:
    A. Yul Brenner without the deep voice
    B. Buddah without the wisdom
    C. Dr. Evil without a Mini-me

16) Bill Veck asked Chicago Cub Merv Connors to do what before he jumped from a hotel ledge:
   A. Rewrite his will to give Bill the power of attorney
   B. Try to avoid hitting Veck's new car parked on the street below
   C. Put on his uniform so the team could get some much-needed publicity

17) Who made Christopher Reeve laugh at a critical time in his recovery?
   A. Billy Crystal
   B. Robin Williams
   C. Boris Karloff

18) Terry Geddes was burned over 60% of his body but he never quit laughing. What was the saying he wore on his T-shirt?
   A. "Ask me about fire safety."
   B. "I'm a hunka-hunka burning love."
   C. "I may look well-done, but I'm a very rare person."

19) When Hank Young was in Vietnam, he said that something cost $25,000. It was:
   A. A toilet
   B. A beer cooler
   C. A bribe to get himself home early

20) As a reaction to Richard's heart medication, he got a permanent:
   A. Election
   B. Erection
   C. Pimpled complexion

SCRAMBLER

Unscramble these sayings and quotes:

1) Naster Family Proverb
het ifylma atth glhsua htrgeeot tfsagr gtreehto

____

2) Rules of Mourning Psalms 30:5
pgwneie yma rrayt het tngih, tbu oyj smcoe hwti eht gnniomr

____

3) Said to Mary Streiff in a mental hospital
yvoreyebd si tnsu ew tsju tgo atchug

____

4) From Amy Fridrich's poem 'Laughing With the World'
uatrgleh si osd'g gsno, ti snirbg su spsaiepnh

____

5) Steve Palermo's inspirational creed
tna'c vrene idd ghtionn

____

THE MATCH GAME

Match the person with the affliction they laughed through:

David Naster	Multiple Sclerosis
Jim O'Hara	Bone, liver, pancreas, back cancer
Steve Palermo	Cerebral Palsy/ADD
Mindy Goldstein	POW camp
Jack Mandlebaum	Breast cancer
Duffy Hutton	Gun shot/paralyzed
Bill Mahoney	Concentration camp
Jenny Ashby	Short, balding & squatty

TRIVIA SCAVENGER HUNT

1) Blake Docking posed as this kind of man during the singing of the national anthem. (six-letter word)

___ ___ ___ ___ ___ ___

2) Bill Mahoney said if he had these, he could roll back to his bed. (seven-letter word)

___ ___ ___ ___ ___ ___ ___

3) EMT Mike Dittamore said these were welcome in the ER any time they could get one. HINT: candy bar! (eight-letter word)

___ ___ ___ ___ ___ ___ ___ ___

4) How much money LeAnn Thieman stuffed in her bra to take to Vietnam to adopt children. (in U.S. dollars)

$ ______________

5) The name of one of the POW camps in Vietnam. (two words; 11 letters total)

___ ___ ___ ___ ___

___ ___ ___ ___ ___ ___

6) Duffy had this made before he became a POW. (two words; 10 letters total)

___ ___ ___ ___

___ ___ ___ ___ ___ ___

7) The color of the last remaining four hairs Barbara Johnson had left on her head after chemo. (four-letter word)

___ ___ ___ ___

8) Cancer survivor, Gary Leezack, said, "It's hard to get sick and die when you know you're going to ... ?" (six-letter word)

____ ____ ____ ____ ____ ____

9) Breast cancer survivor, Dick Schulte, lost three of these in one week. (five-letter word)

____ ____ ____ ____ ____

10) Fell out and onto senior woman's lap from laughing so hard. (five-letter word)

____ ____ ____ ____ ____

11) Big Dale Wright got stung by a bee riding on this. (10-letter word)

___ ___ ___ ___ ___ ___ ___ ___ ___ ___

12) Special Olympic's cheer to football team. (five-letter word)

____ ____ ____ ____ ____

13) Double amputee, Dick Solowitz, planned one-man stage show named ... (seven-letter word)

____ ____ ____ ____ ____ ____ ____

14) Australian, Jack Newton, walked into a moving airplane's what? (nine-letter word)

____ ____ ____ ____ ____ ____ ____ ____ ____

15) Norm Alden was staring into this when he woke from a nap. (seven-letter word)

____ ____ ____ ____ ____ ____ ____

16) Chris to Swiss got stabbed this many times. (seven-letter word)

____ ____ ____ ____ ____ ____ ____

17) Friend of Jack Mandlebaum's who survived Nazi concentration camp. (six-letter word)

____ ____ ____ ____ ____ ____

18) Richard Stern's doctor (also the name of a Steely Dan song). (two-letter word)

____ ____

19) In the Great Pizza Caper, four paralyzed patients snuck out to get pizza. How many pizzas did they order? (three-letter word)

____ ____ ____

The nurses who caught the Pizza Team suggested this as punishment. (eight-letter word)

____ ____ ____ ____ ____ ____ ____ ____

20) Game passed between friends after erection room visit. (two words; eight letters total)

____ ____ ____ ____   ____ ____ ____ ____

ANSWER KEY

Answers to Multiple Choice

1 .... A	6 ..... A	11 .... B	16 C
2 .... A	7 ..... B	12 .... B	17 .... B
3 .... A	8 ..... B	13 .... B	18 .... B
4 C	9 C	14 .... B	19 .... B
5 C	10 C	15 .... B	20 .... B

Answers to the Scrambler

1) Naster Family Proverb
   The family that laughs together grafts together.
2) Rules of Mourning Psalms 30:5
   Weeping may tarry the night, but joy comes with the morning.
3) Said to Mary Streiff in a mental hospital
   Everybody is nuts. We just got caught.
4) From Amy Fridrich's poem 'Laughing With the World'
   Laughter is God's song, it brings us happiness.
5) Steve Palermo's inspirational creed
   Can't never did nothing.

Answers to the Match Game

Jim O'Hara	Multiple Sclerosis
Steve Palermo	Gun shot/paralyzed
Mindy Goldstein	Cerebral Palsy/ADD
Jack Mandlebaum	Concentration camp
Duffy Hutton	POW camp
Bill Mahoney	Bone, liver, pancreas, back cancer
Jenny Ashby	Breast cancer

Answers to Trivia Scavenger Hunt

1) MUSCLE	11) MOTORCYCLE
2) CASTORS	12) NORMY
3) SNICKERS	13) STUMPED
4) $10,000	14) PROPELLER
5) HANOI HILTON	15) SHOTGUN
6) BELT BUCKLE	16) SIXTEEN
7) GRAY	17) MONIEK
8) HAWAII	18) WU
9) BOOBS	19) SIX; GROUNDED
10) TEETH	20) RING TOSS

Who is David Naster?

And what exactly has he done?

David Naster has been making people laugh for over 23 years. From his numerous national television shows to his feature presentations on HBO, Showtime, The Arts & Entertainment channel, and the prestigious award of *National College Comedian of the Year*, David knows how to tickle human beings' funny bone.

He has been responsible for literally millions of laughs on three continents, two hemispheres, 50 states, 526 college campuses and all of the major comedy nightclubs in the United States.

Toll Free: 888/815-8119 • Fax: 913/438-4870
www.naster.com

David also spreads laughter throughout the corporate community. A partial list of his corporate clients include:

AT&T	IBM
ShowTime	Kodak
WalMart	Fox Television Network
NBC	Children's Television Network
Sprint	BBC
Coca-Cola	Anheuser-Busch
CBS	ABC
HBO	Coors Brewing Company
MTV	Union Pacific/Southern Railroad

State Farm Insurance
Kansas City Life Insurance
Southwestern Bell
Southern New England Bell
National Football League (NFL)
Paine-Webber
Authur-Andersen
Phillip Morris
Paramount Studios
Universal Studios
Norwegian Cruise Lines
Yellow Freight
Central Intelligence Agency of the United States

"You Just Have To Laugh"

•• Comes to You ••

David Naster travels all over the world making people laugh and would like to visit your corner of the world. His "You Just Have To Laugh" presentation shows us the value and power of humor and laughing in our daily life as well as work place.

You'll laugh, you'll smile, you might even shed a heart felt tear, as David shares with you how fellow human beings have laughed their way through life's greatest challenges. He will give you the tools to expand your "Humorous Perspective" in all facets of your life.

The true heart of David's presentations is the everyday things we all encounter and how to appreciate their humorous angles. David Naster speaks to Fortune 500 companies, professional associations, government agencies (the CIA included), religious groups and small businesses. He welcomes any group of human beings who want and need to laugh. (He is still working on other species.)

Toll Free: 888/815-8119 • Fax: 913/438-4870
www.naster.com

Have You Just Had to Laugh?

If you have any true stories how you or someone you know have used humor and laughing, please let David know. Here are some of the categories he is needing stories for:

You Just Have To Laugh:

At relationships; spouses, friends and dating

At your relatives and family

At growing up: childhood, adolescence and adulthood

At parenting

At recovery, illness and addiction

At your job

At teaching; how educators use humor

Please feel free to contact David Naster
at any of the following:

Toll Free: 888/815-8119 • Fax: 913/438-4870
www.naster.com

You Just Have to Laugh

USING HUMOR TO MAKE TOUGH TIMES BETTER

AND

You Just Have to Laugh ... Again

HOW TO LAUGH WHEN LIFE ISN'T FUNNY

David Naster

... are now available on CD. Also on cassette tape is David Naster's hysterical comedy routine titled, "Surf and Turf." Half recorded on land, the other on a cruise ship, the laughs never stop.

All three recordings are perfect to listen to when you're stuck in traffic, on a long commute, facing airport delays or when "You Just Need to Laugh." These recordings will have you laughing out loud and can be ordered by contacting any of the following:

Toll Free: 888/815-8119 • Fax: 913/438-4870
www.naster.com

You Just Have to Laugh

COMEDY WORKBOOK

- Learn how to be funny
- Learn how to make your work place funny
- Learn how to make your life funny
- Learn how to deal with "hecklers"
- Learn how to develop your sense of humor

Most self-help books only tell you what to do. The "You Just Have To Laugh" Comedy Workbook shows you, with simple step-by-step instruction, how to do it. Do what? Be funny. Because that's the premise, babe.

"I'll make your life funny, if you send me the money!"

– David Naster

Toll Free: 888/815-8119 • Fax: 913/438-4870
www.naster.com

You Just Have to Laugh

Quick Order Form

There are three ways to order up some laughs:

Call toll-free: 1-888/815-8119 ***or***
E-mail David at www.naster.com ***or***
Use the form below to fax your order

Please call for current prices and shipping & handling fees

FAX FORM

Name

Address

City State Zip

Daytime Telephone Fax Number

Item	Quantity
YOU JUST HAVE TO LAUGH ... AGAIN – book	
YOU JUST HAVE TO LAUGH – book	
YOU JUST HAVE TO LAUGH ... AGAIN – audio book (available on CD only)	
YOU JUST HAVE TO LAUGH – audio book (available on CD or cassette tape)	
YOU JUST HAVE TO LAUGH Comedy Workbook	
SURF AND TURF COMEDY TAPE – cassette	

Toll Free: 888/815-8119 • Fax: 913/438-4870
www.naster.com

Comedy Doodle Page

Use the above space to jot down the page numbers of your favorite stories in the book. Maybe you could write a letter or doodle or even draw funny faces. Hey, how about that grocery list you've been forgetting to make?

(Writing utensil not included.)

You Just Have to Laugh

Quick Order Form

There are three ways to order up some laughs:

Call toll-free: 1-888/815-8119 **OR**
E-mail David at www.naster.com **OR**
Use the form below to fax your order

Please call for current prices and shipping & handling fees

FAX FORM

Name

Address

City State Zip

Daytime Telephone Fax Number

Item	Quantity
YOU JUST HAVE TO LAUGH ... AGAIN – book	
YOU JUST HAVE TO LAUGH – book	
YOU JUST HAVE TO LAUGH ... AGAIN – audio book (available on CD only)	
YOU JUST HAVE TO LAUGH – audio book (available on CD or cassette tape)	
YOU JUST HAVE TO LAUGH Comedy Workbook	
SURF AND TURF COMEDY TAPE – cassette	

Toll Free: 888/815-8119 • Fax: 913/438-4870
www.naster.com